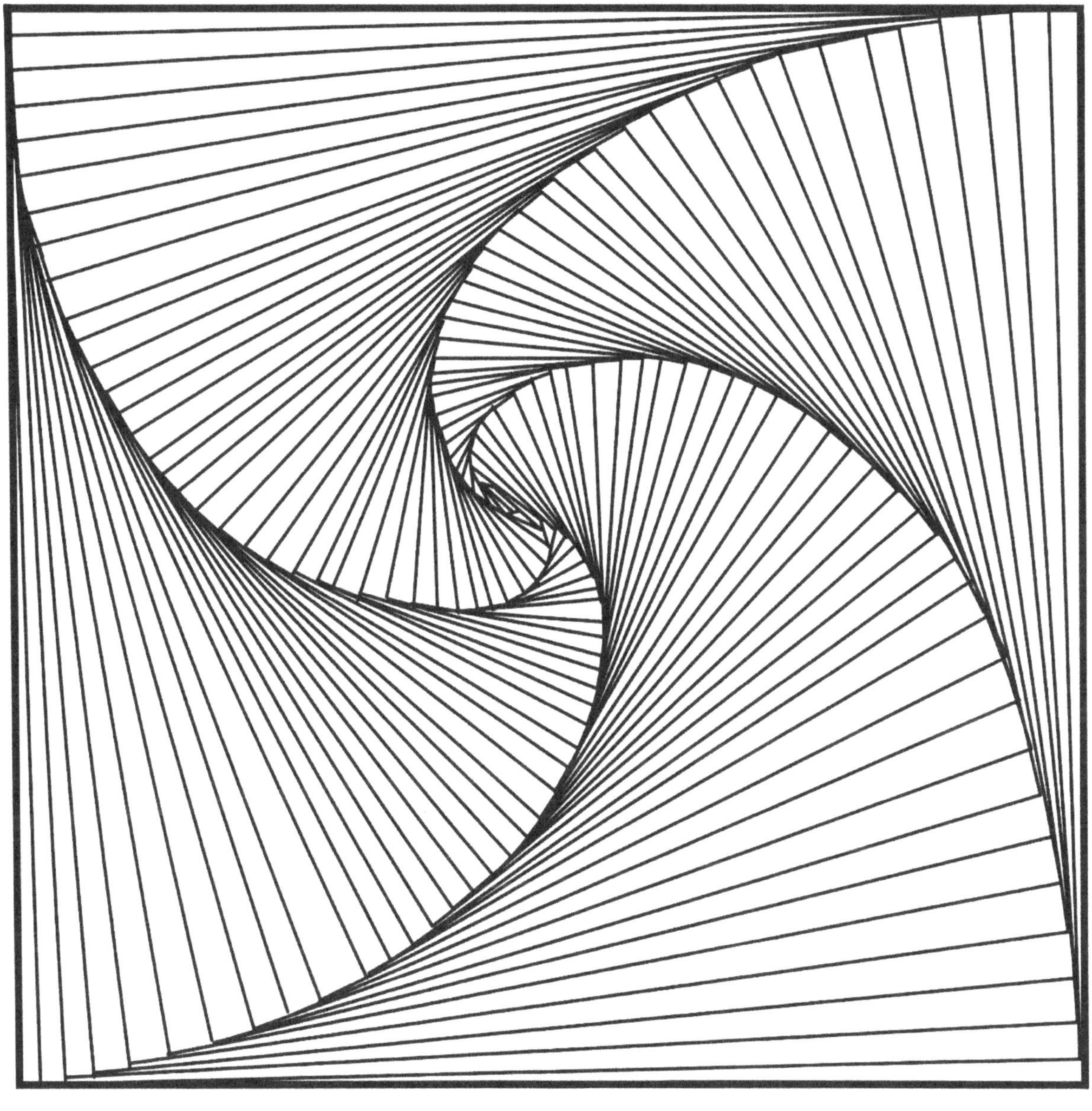

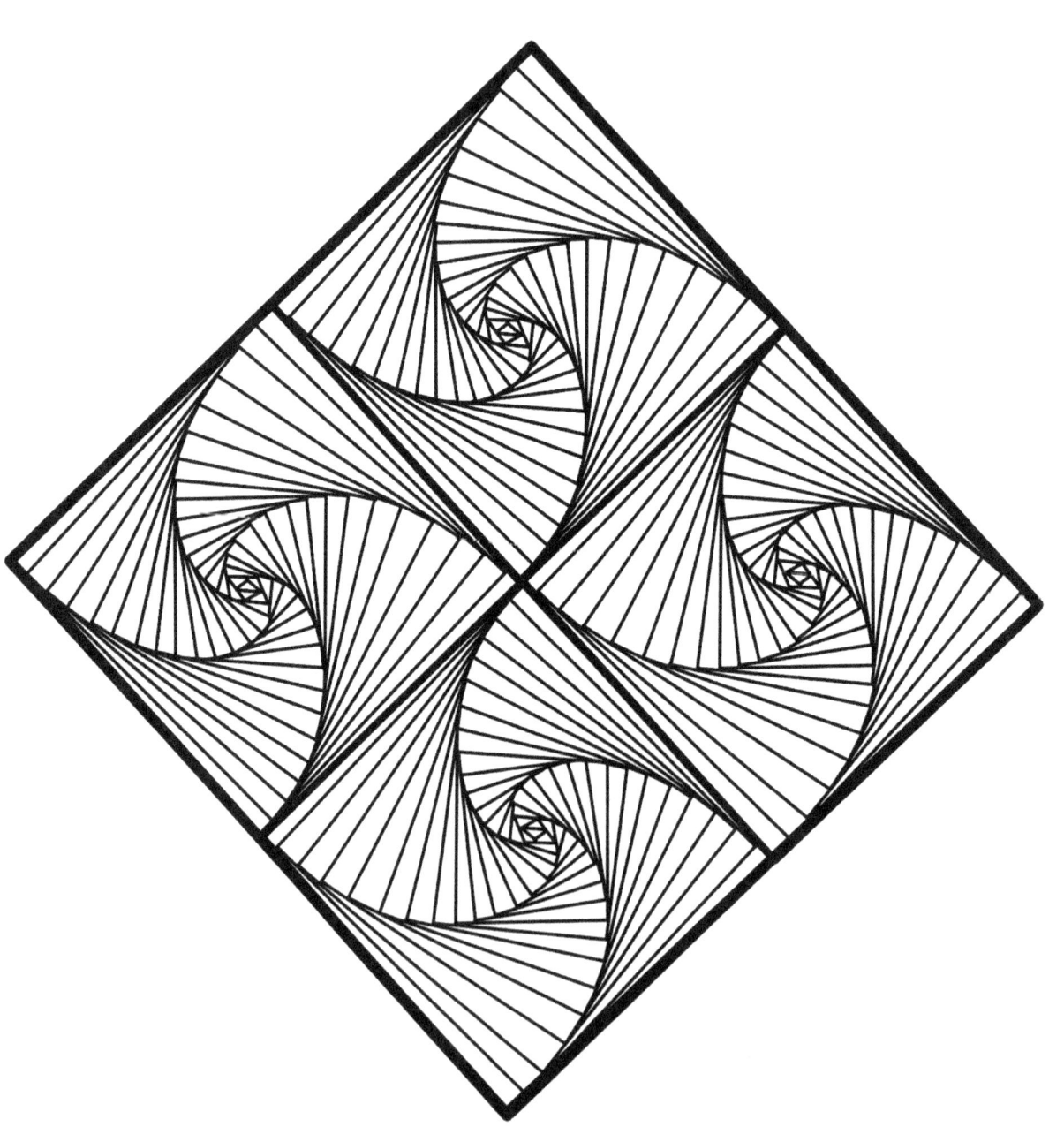

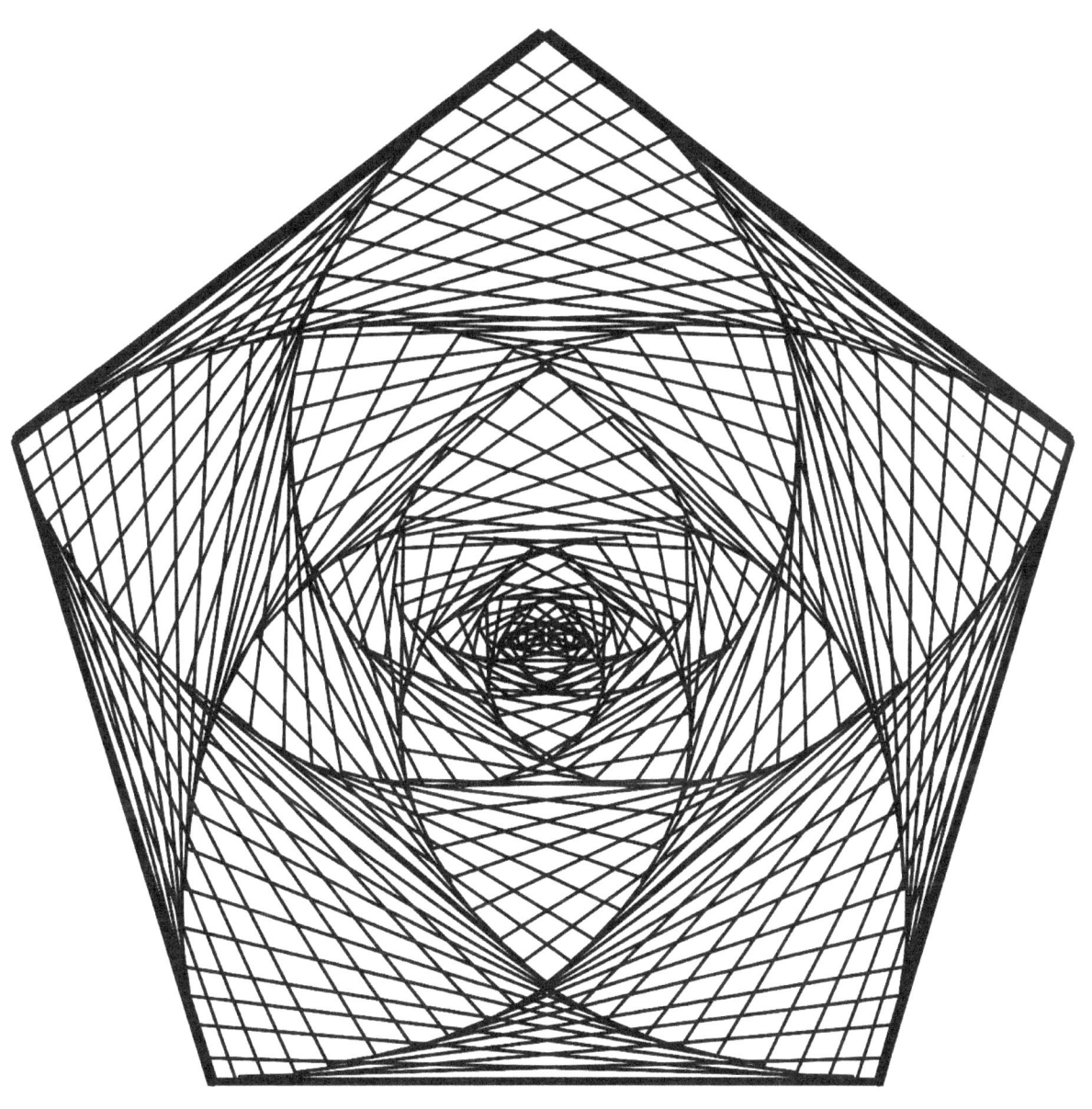

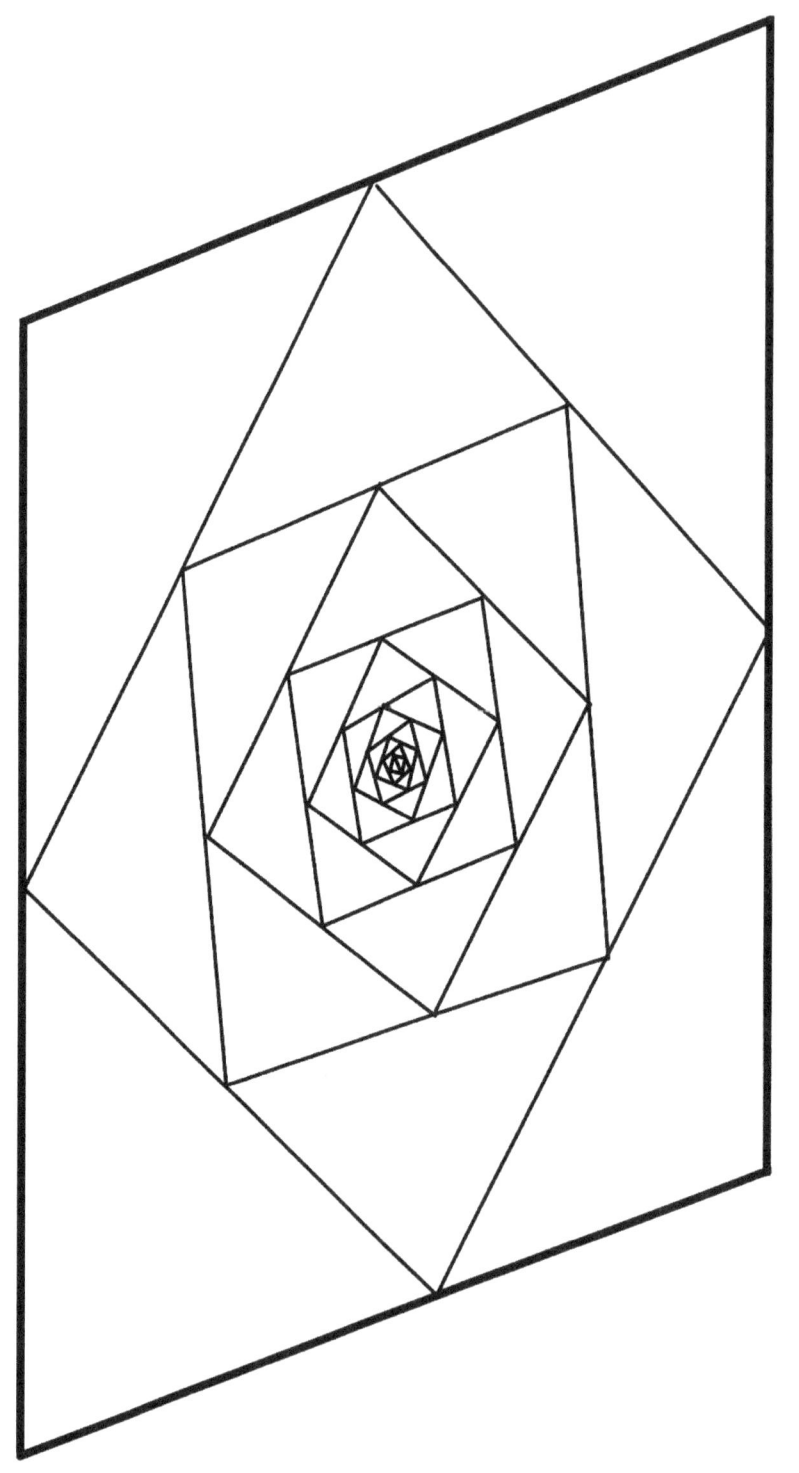

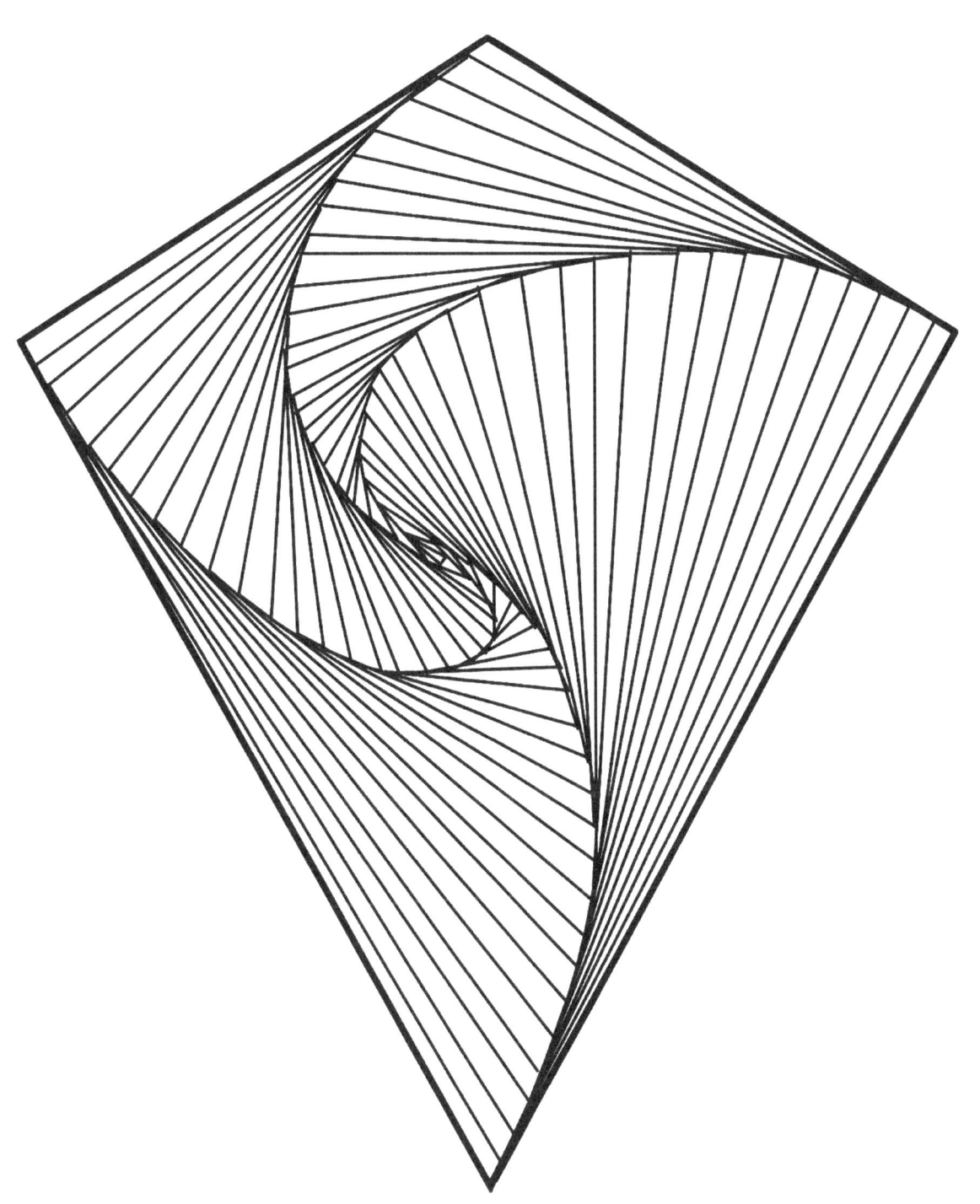

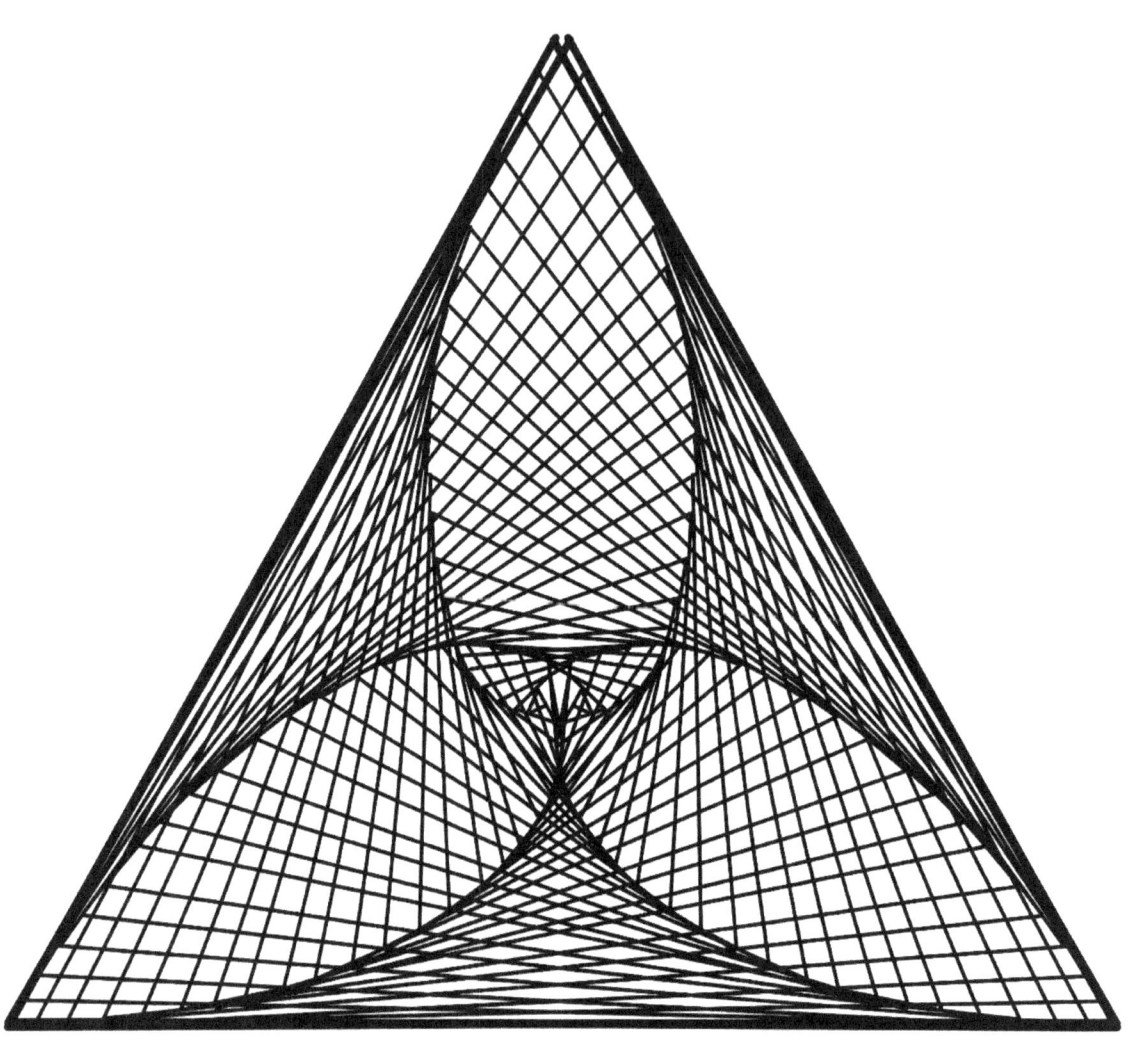

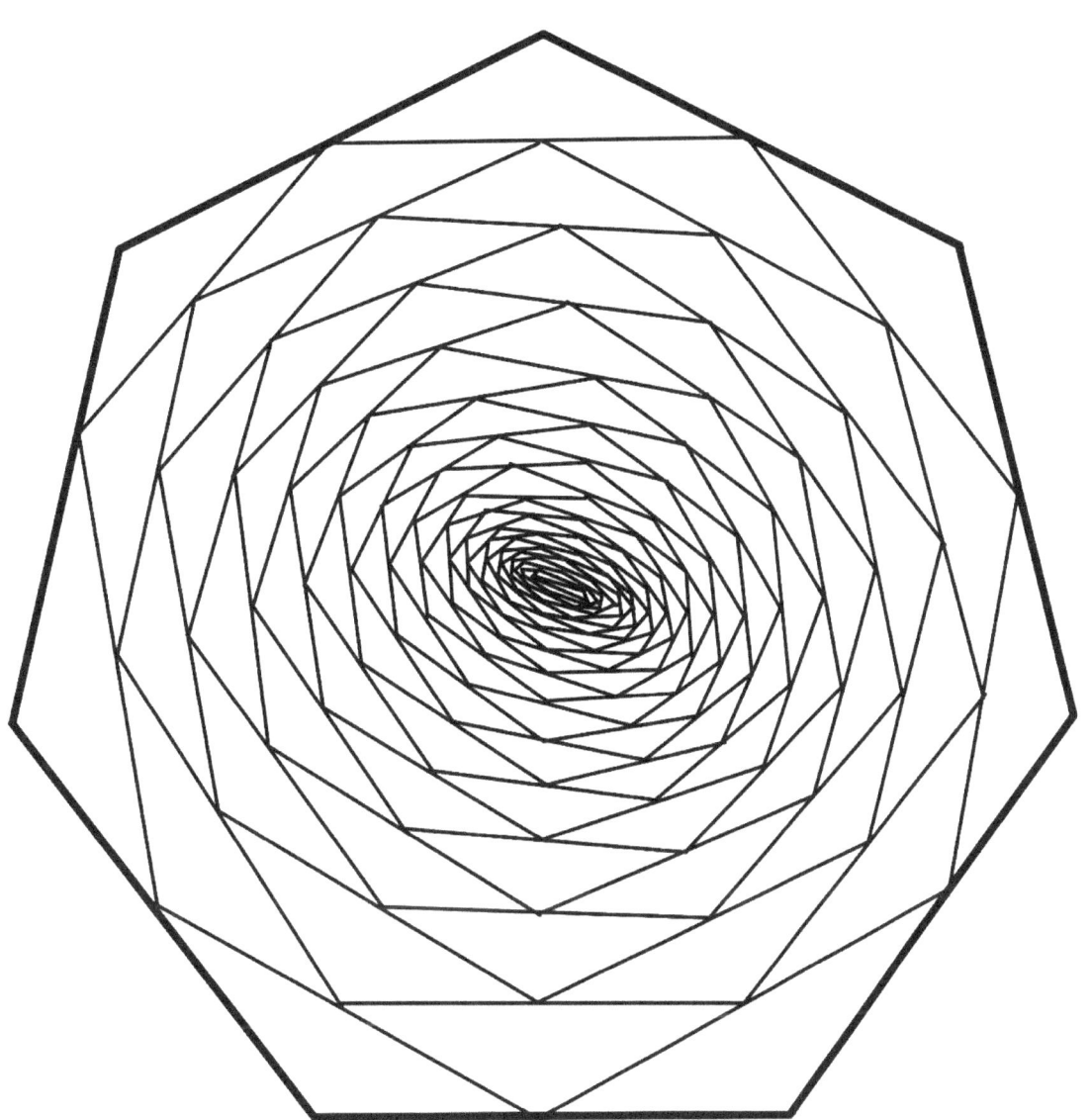

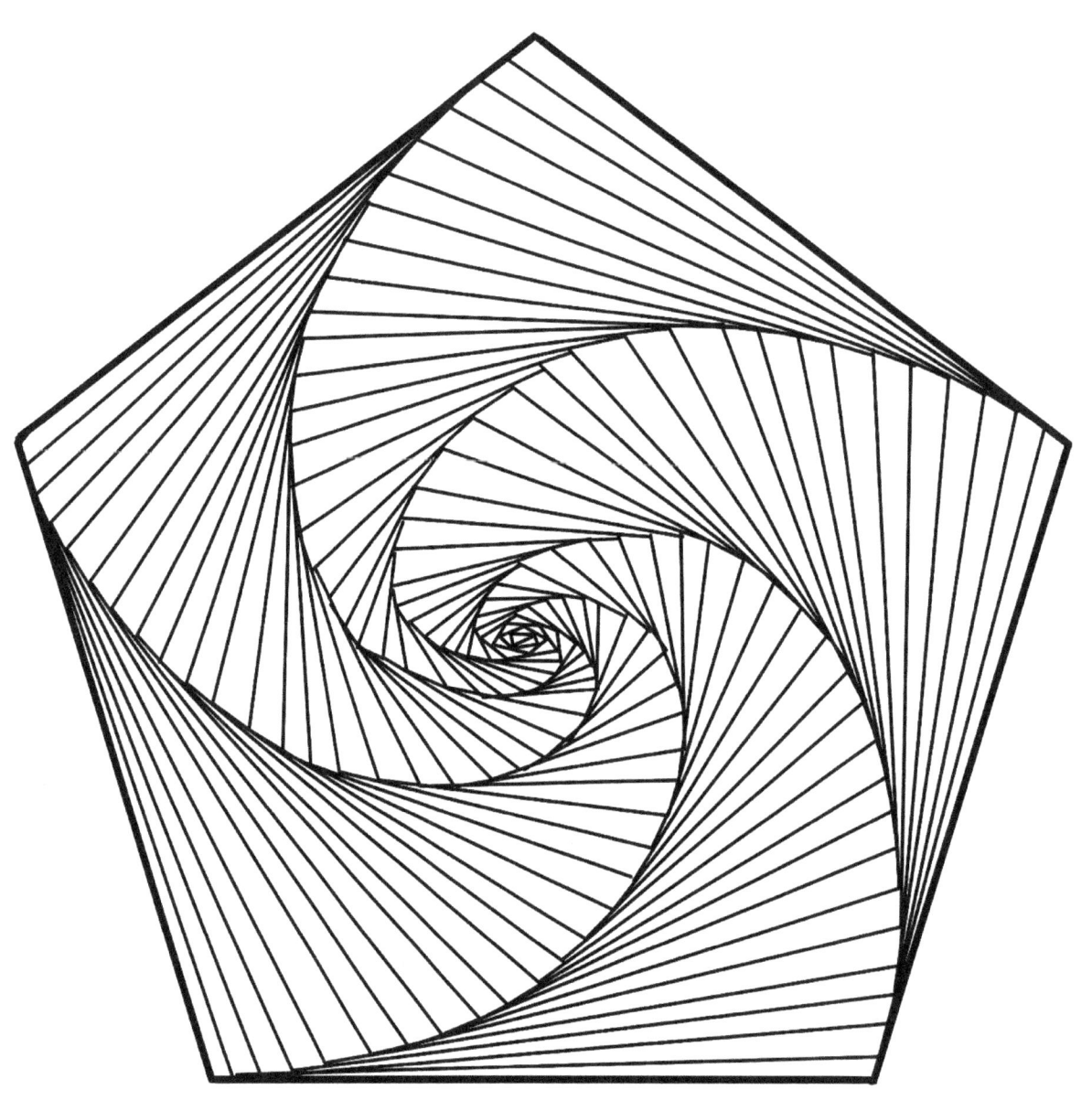

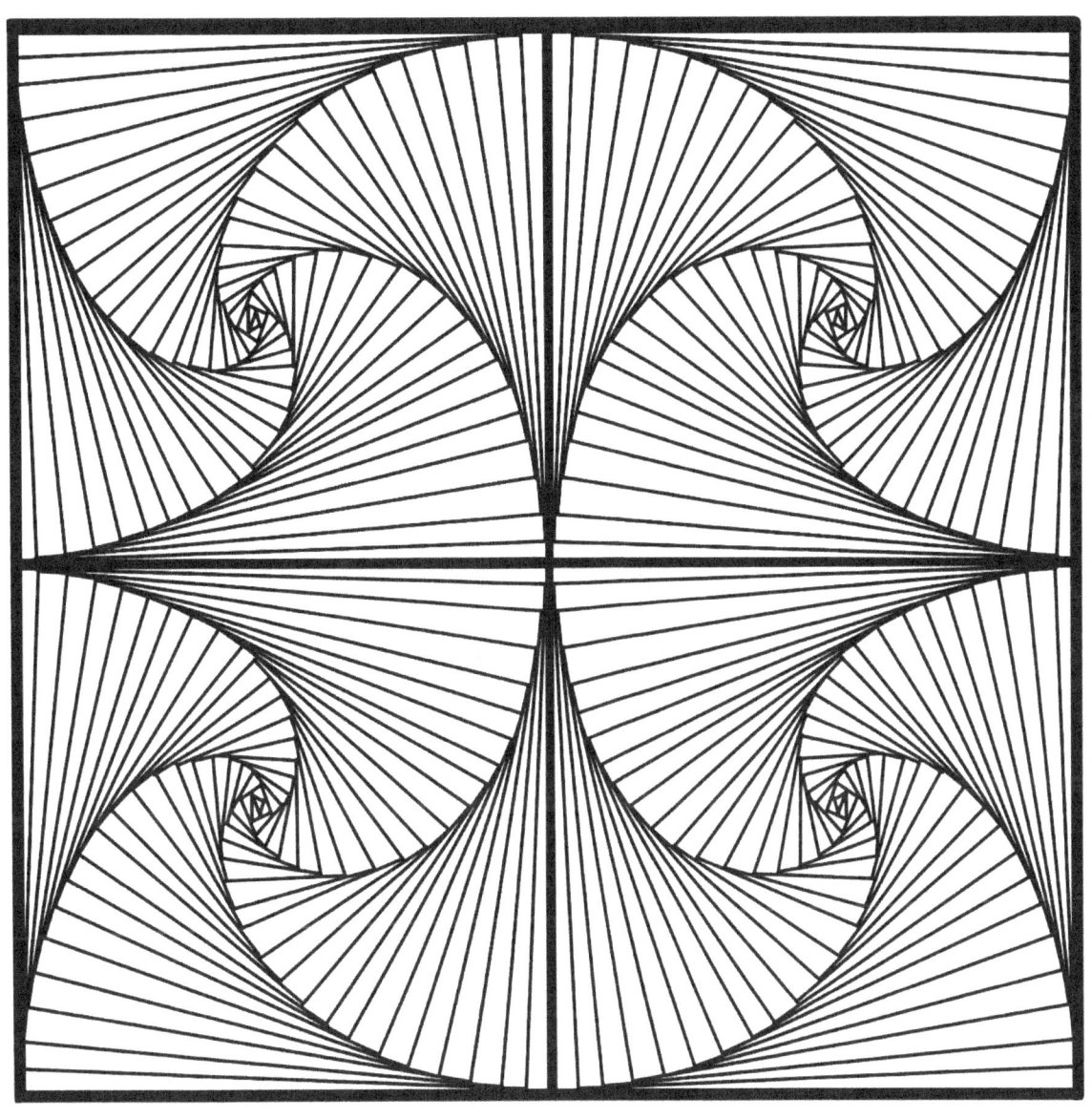

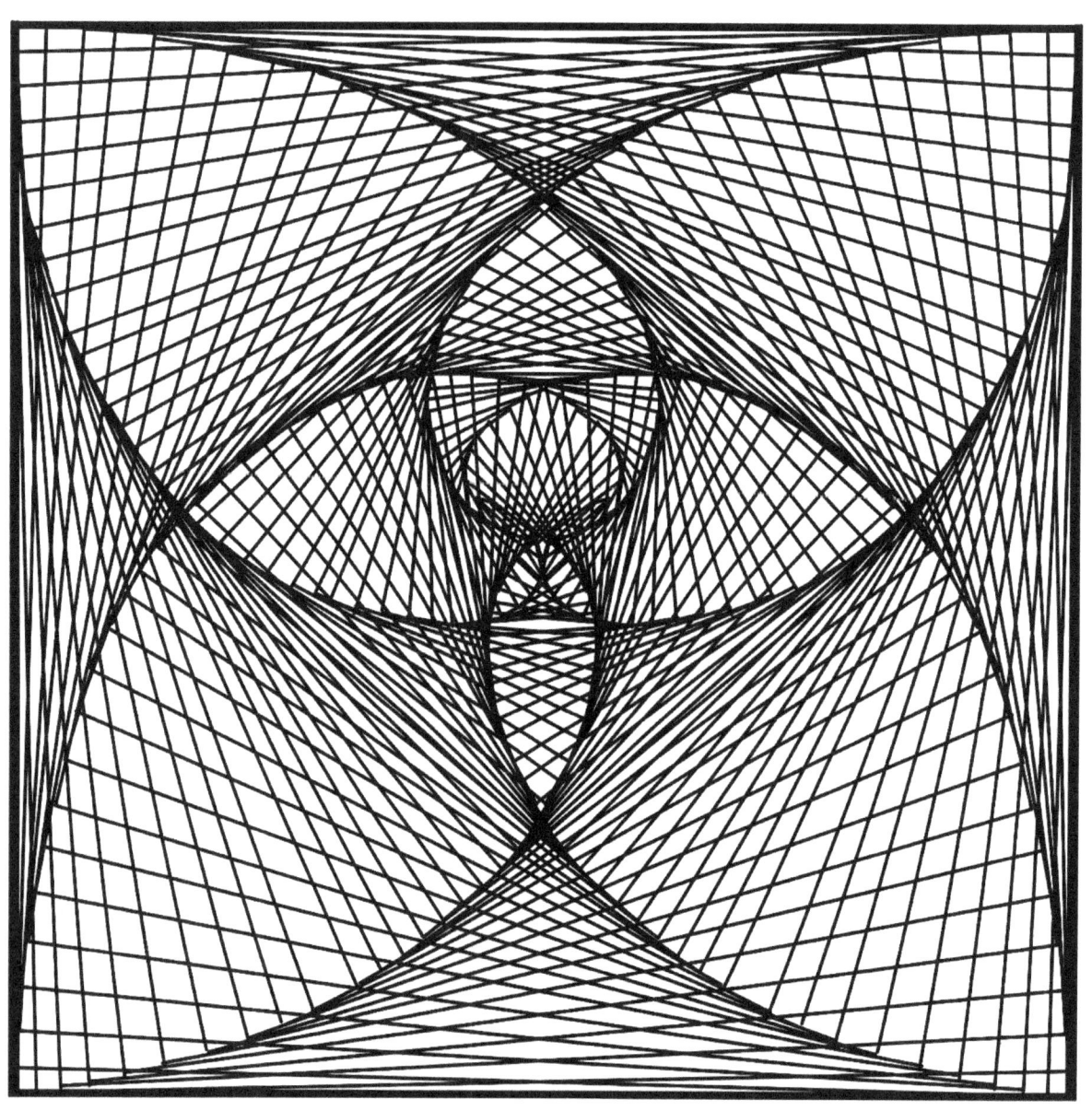

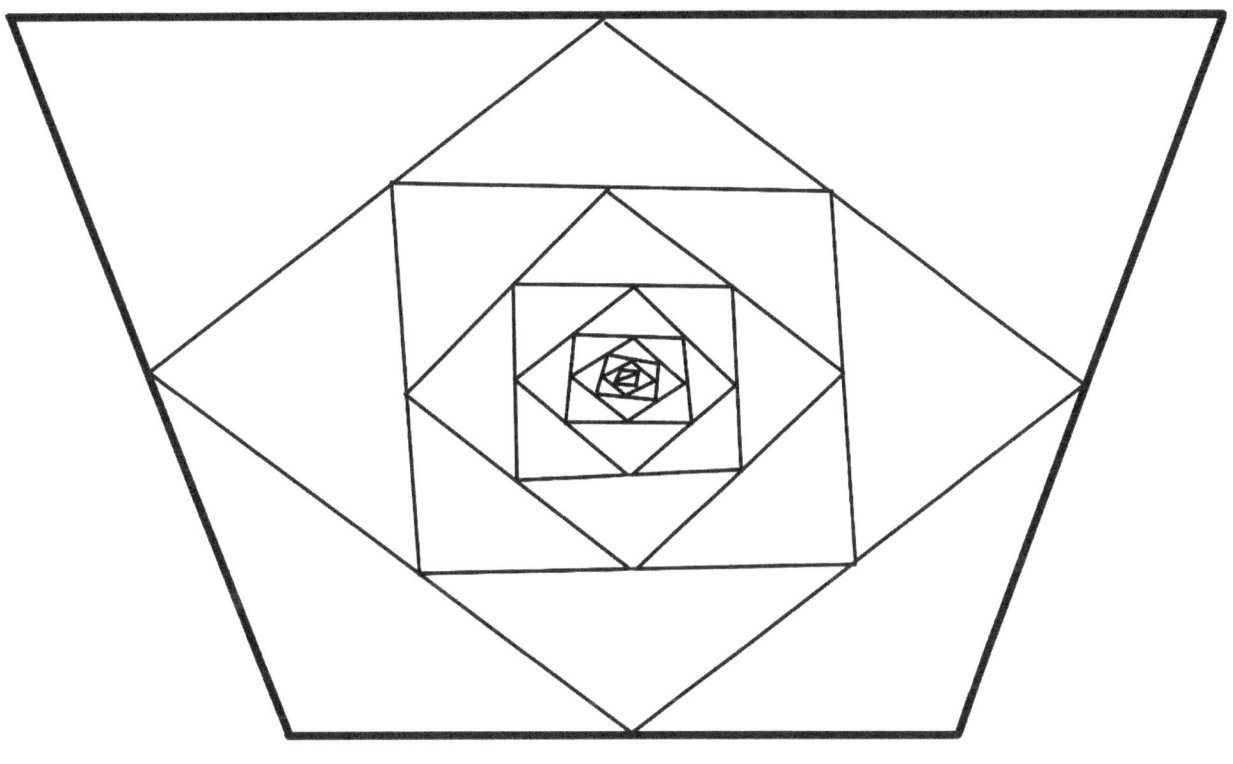

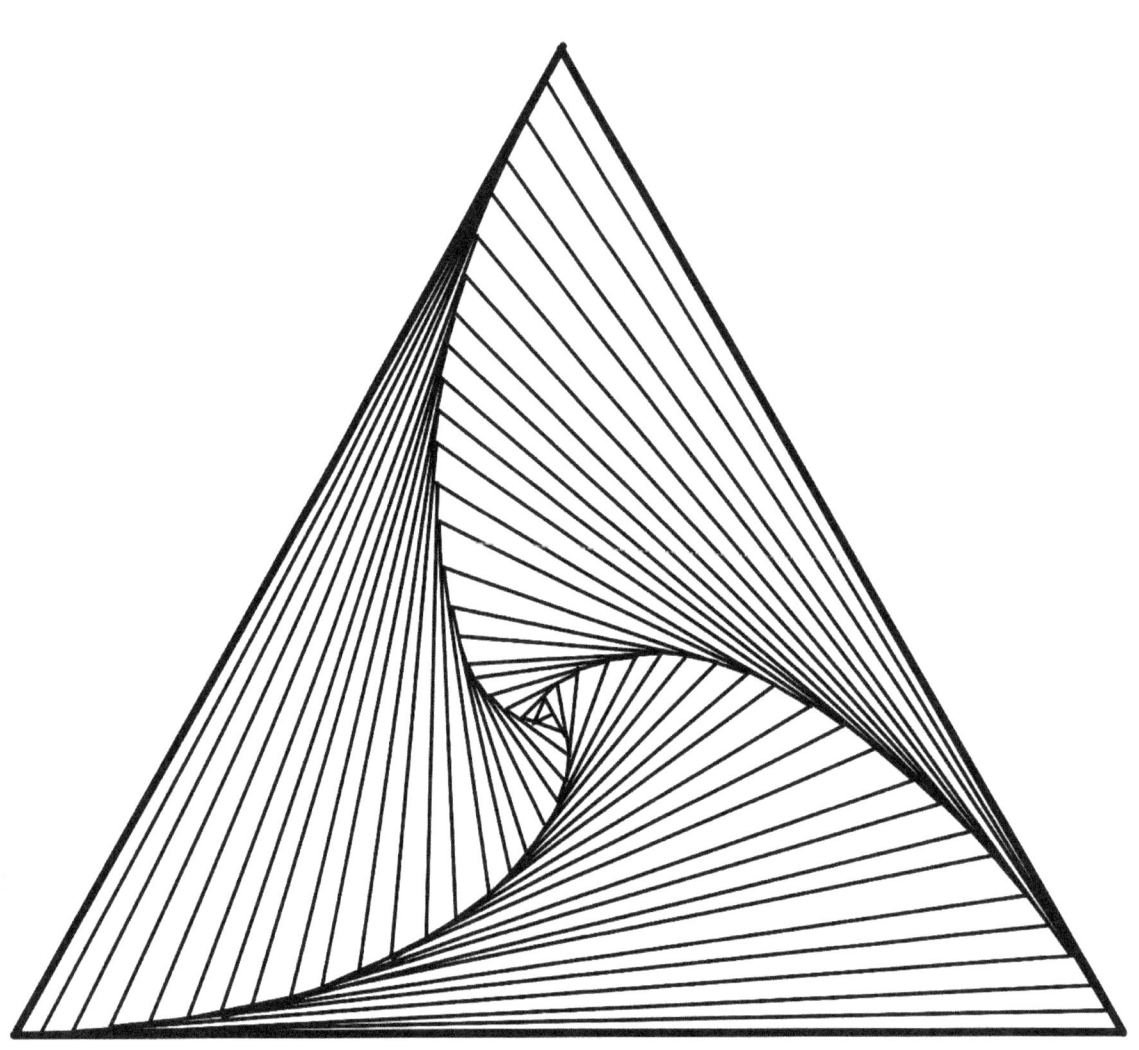

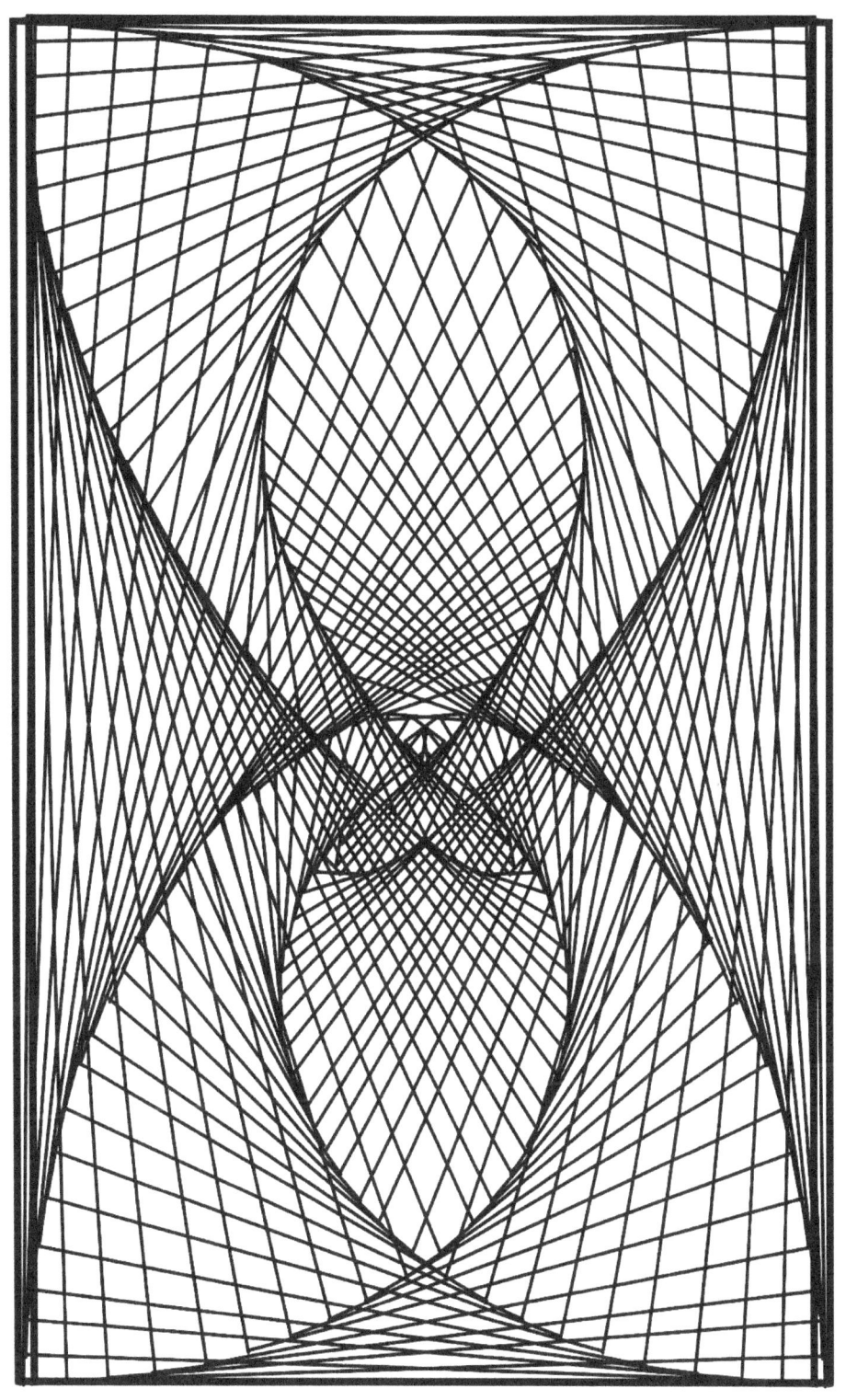

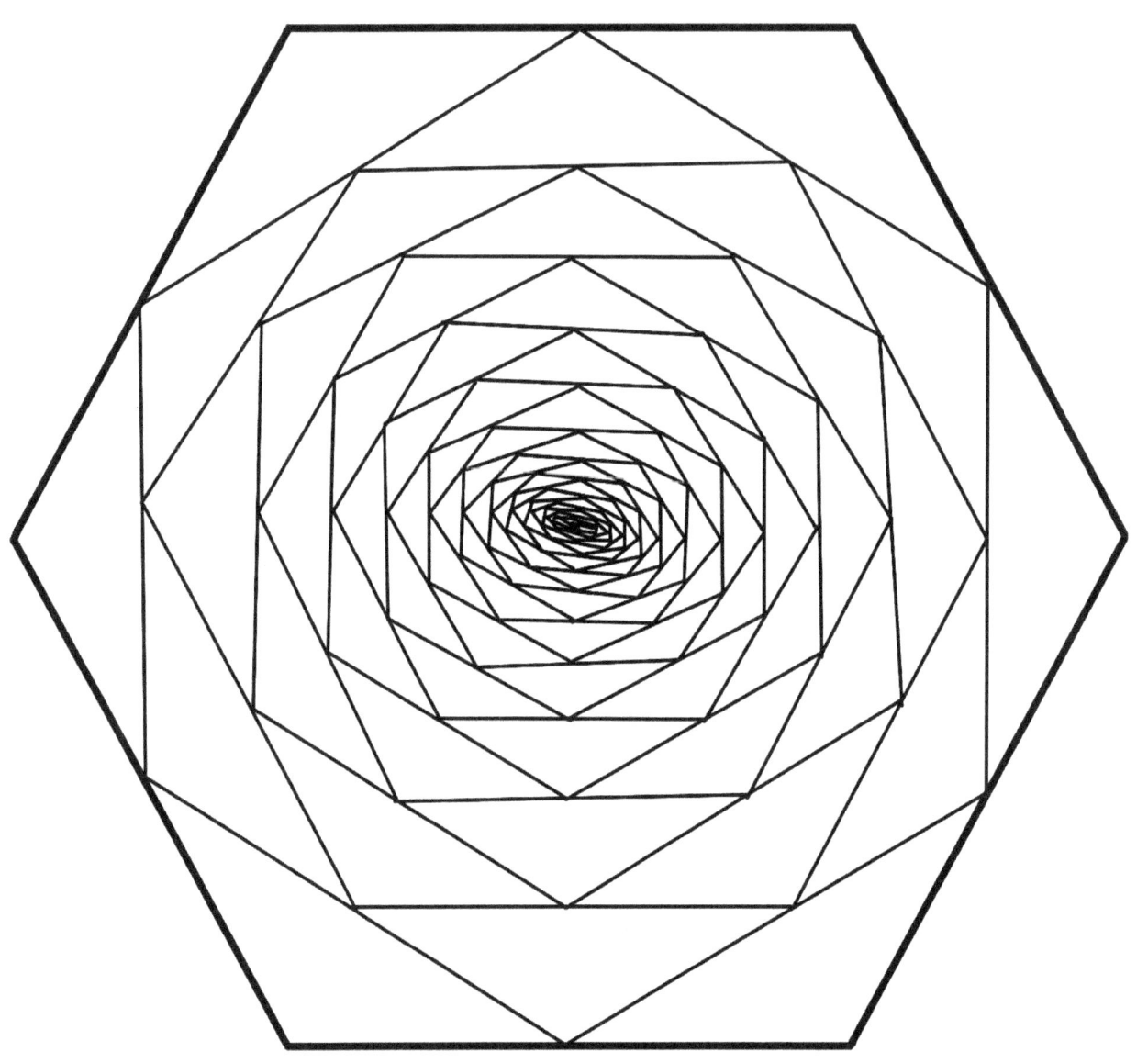

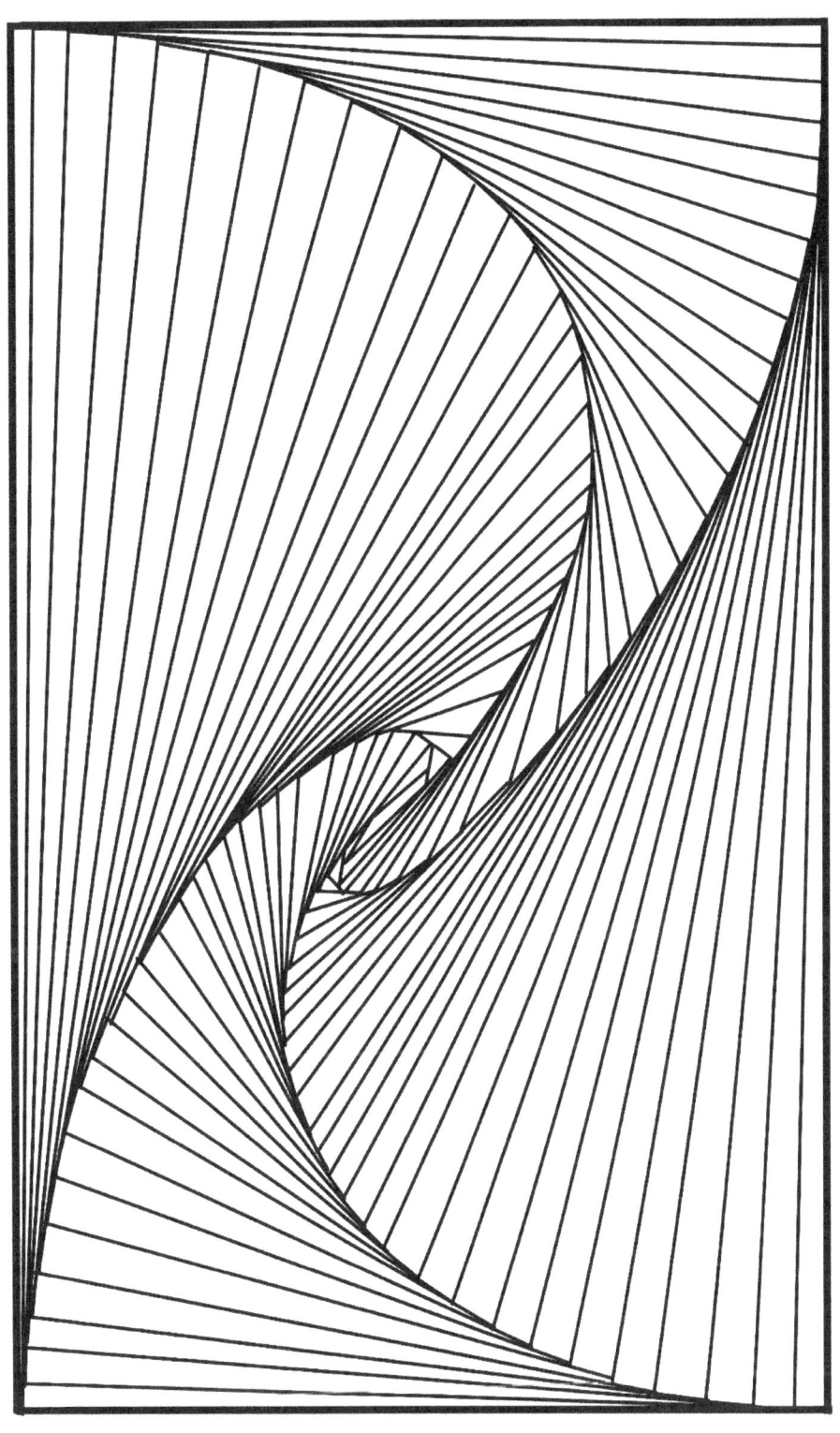

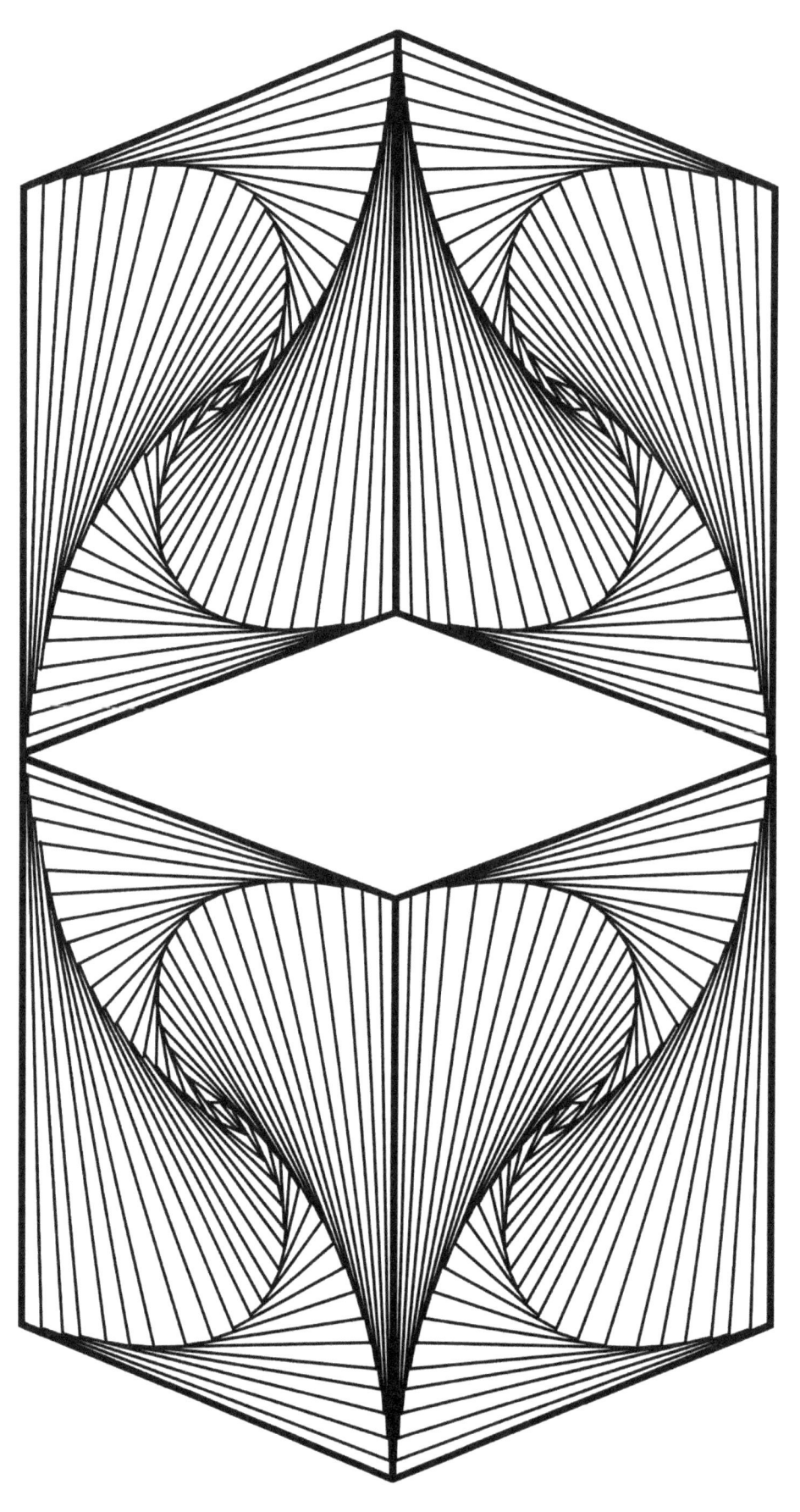

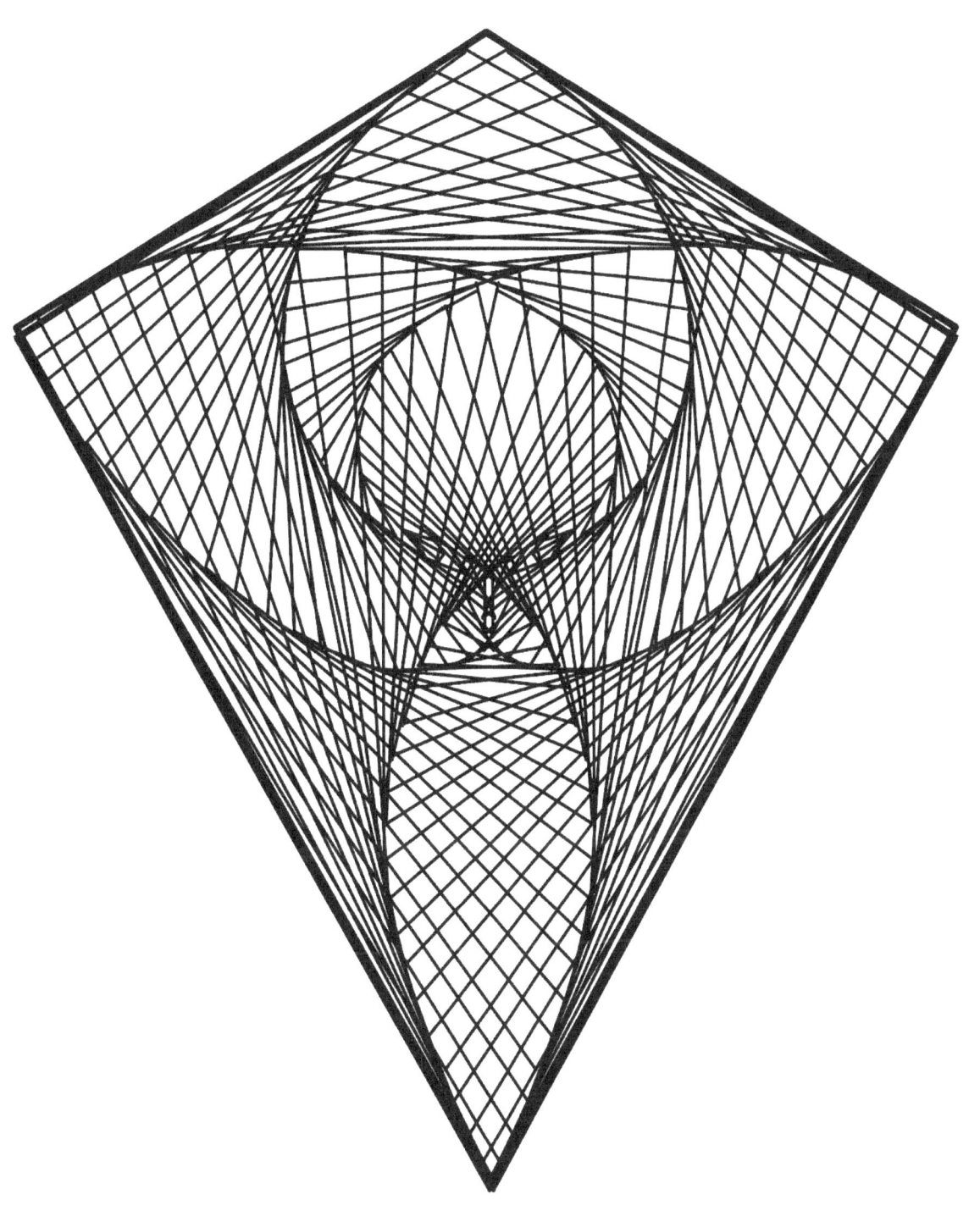

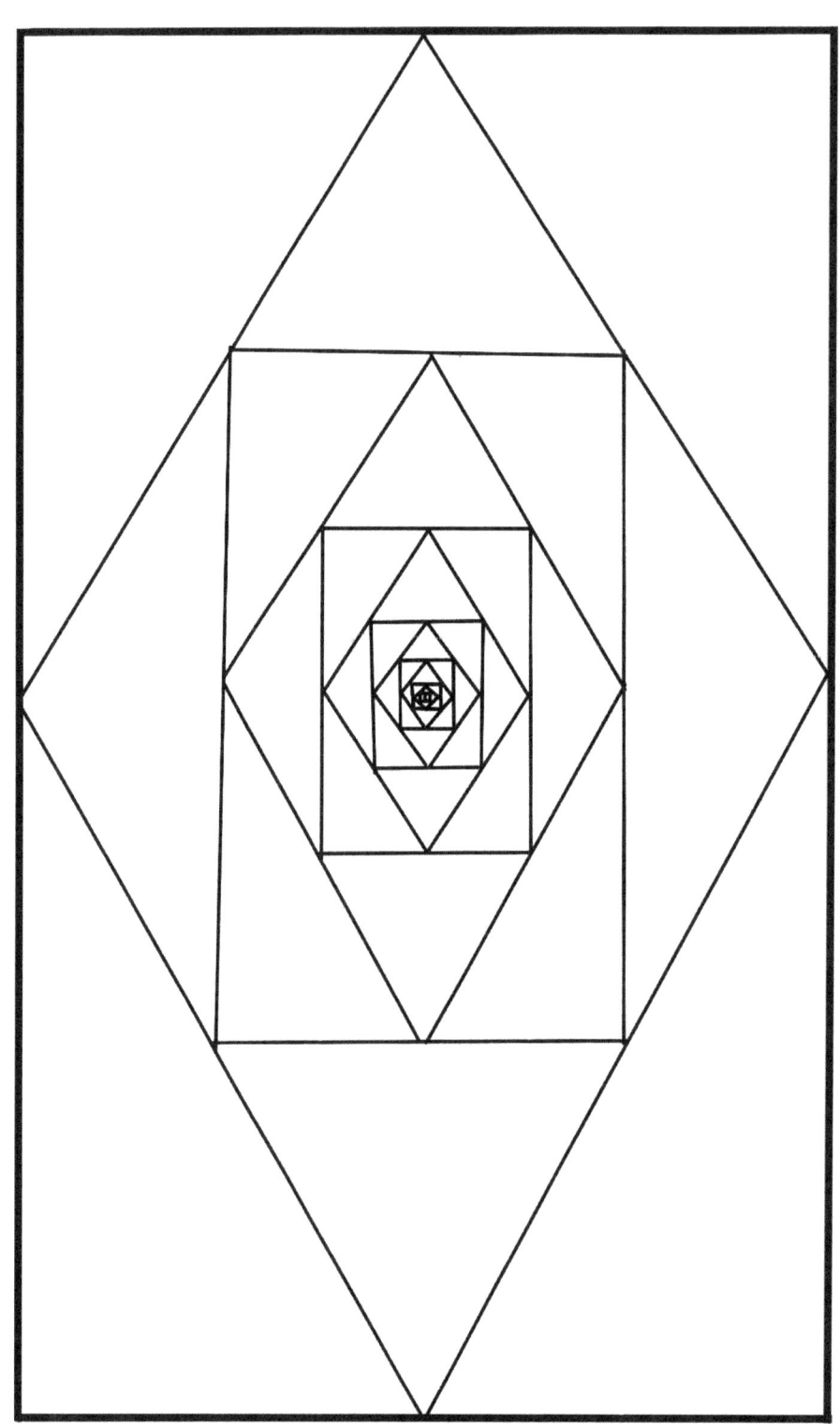

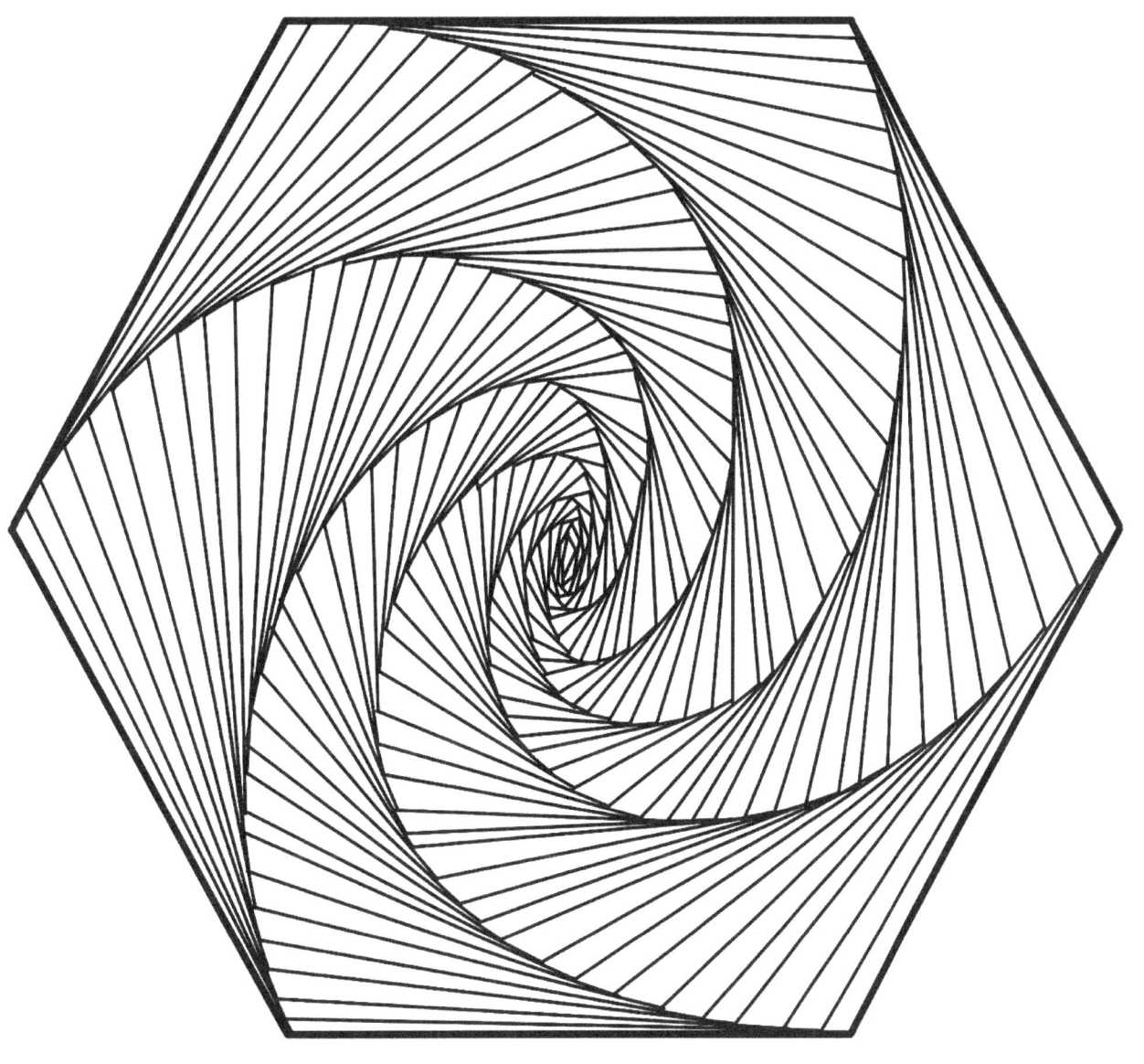

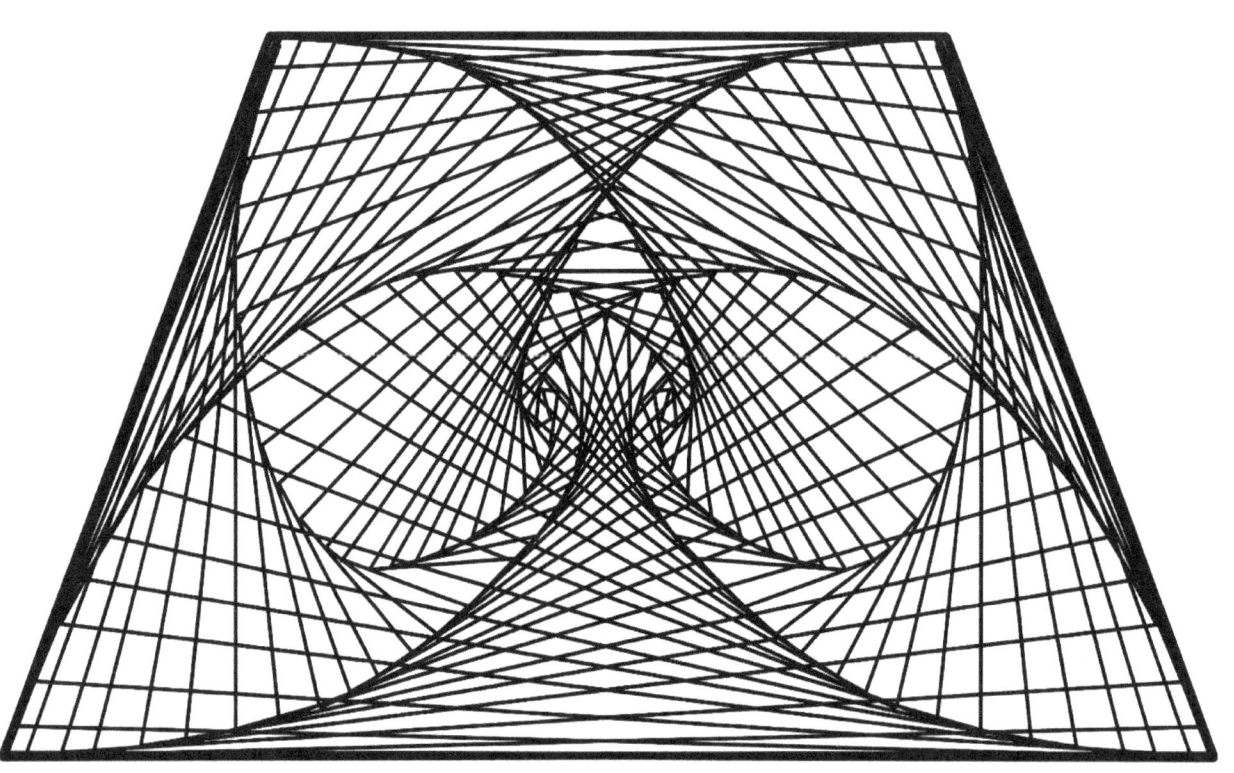

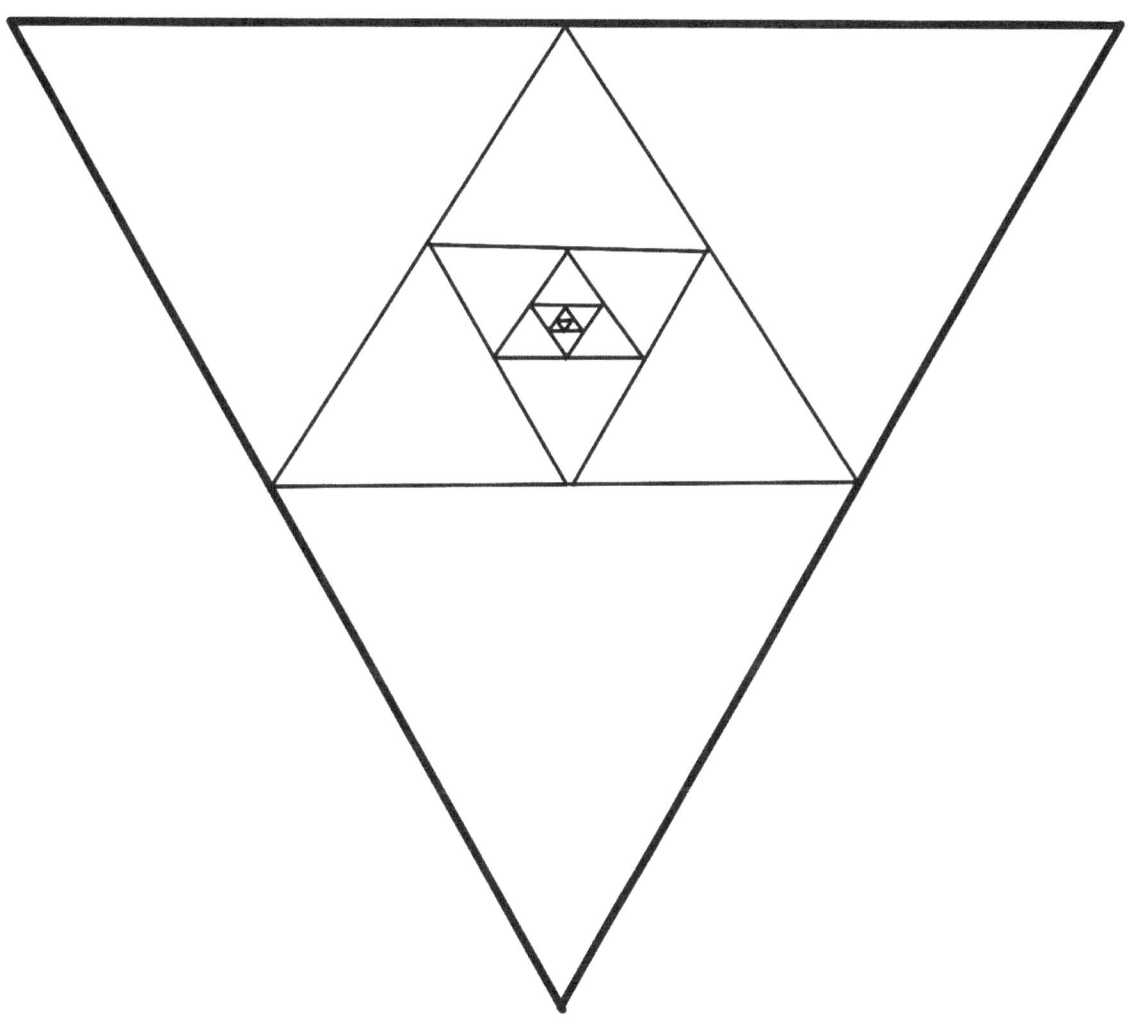

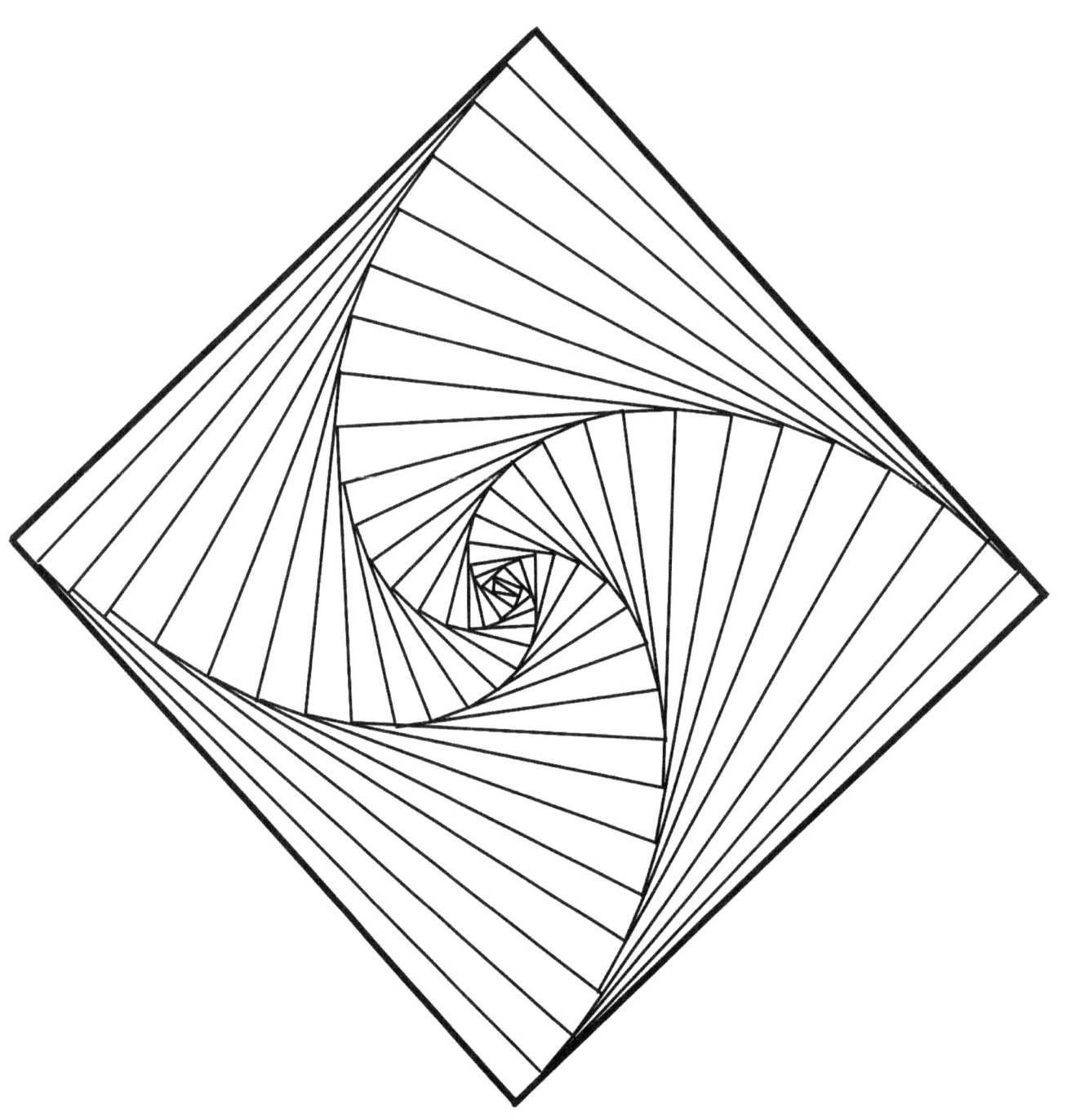

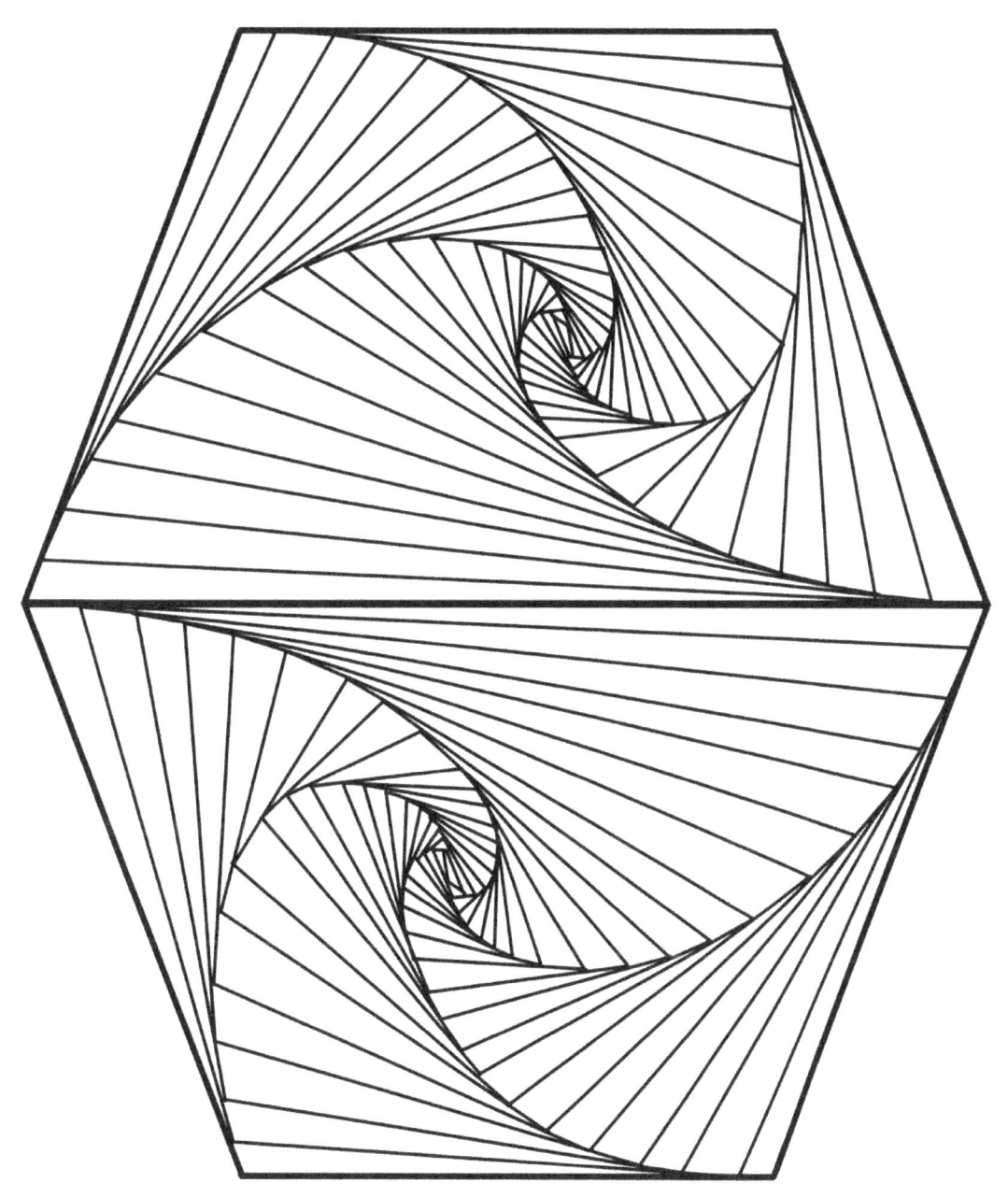

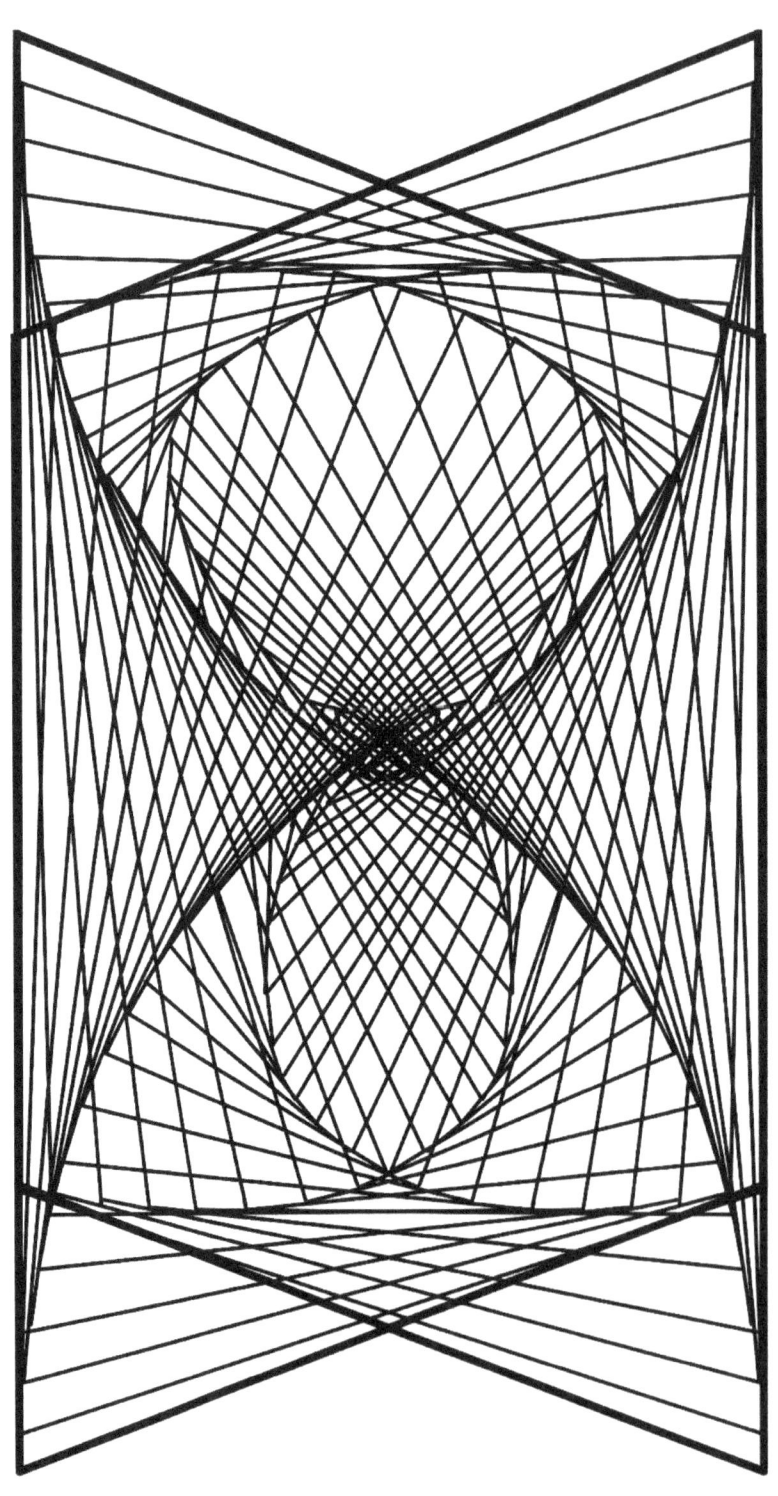

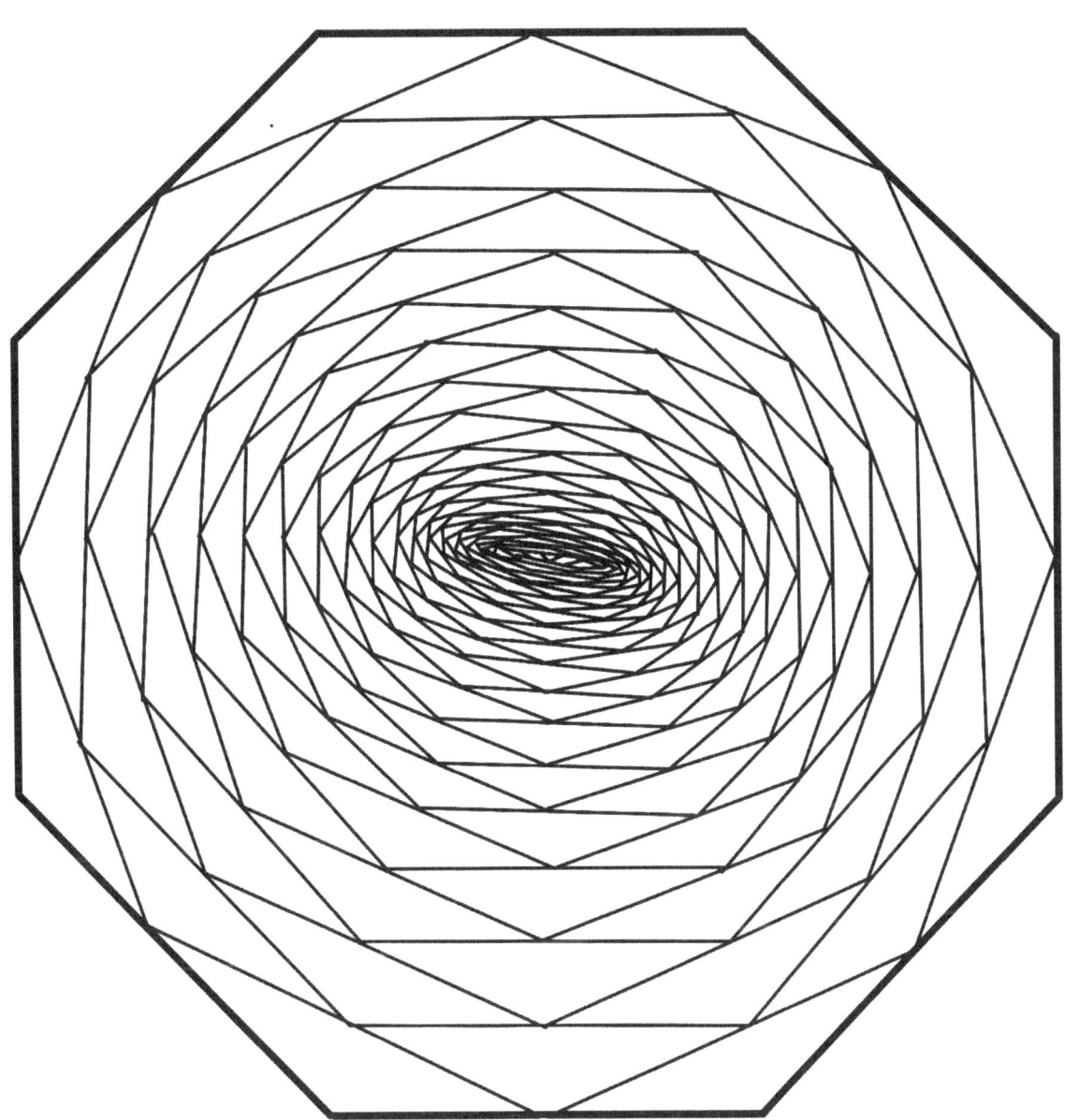

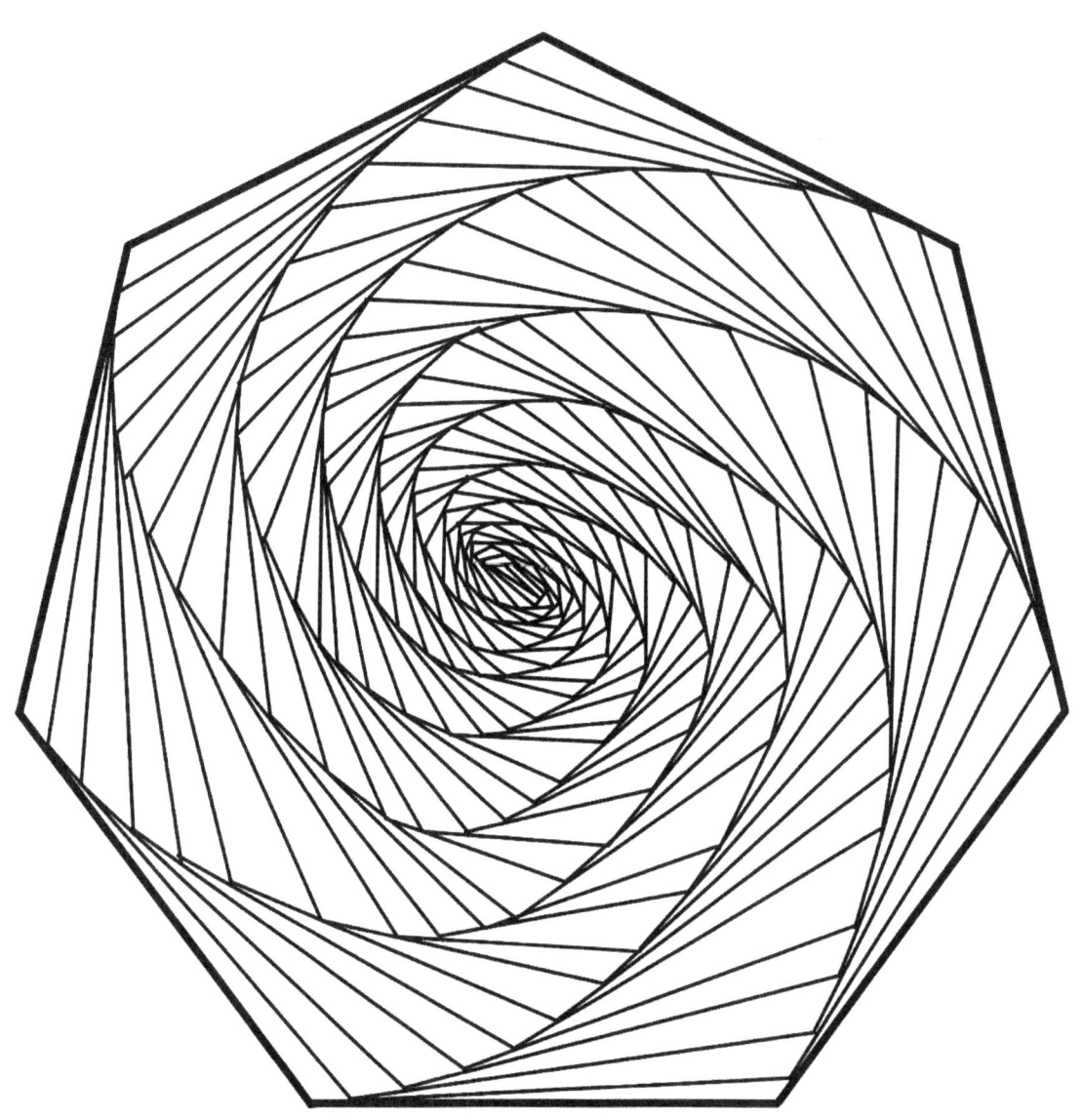

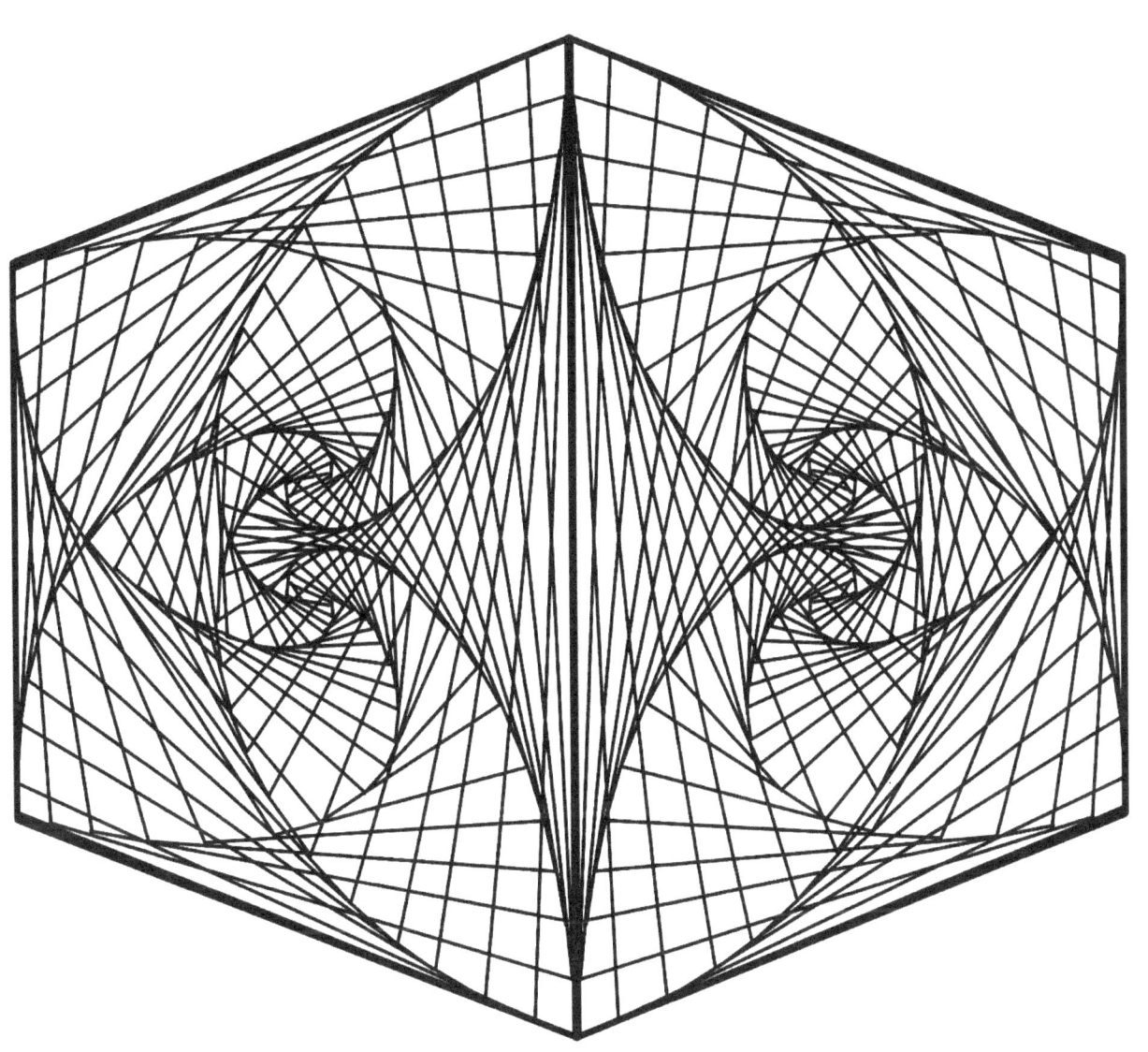

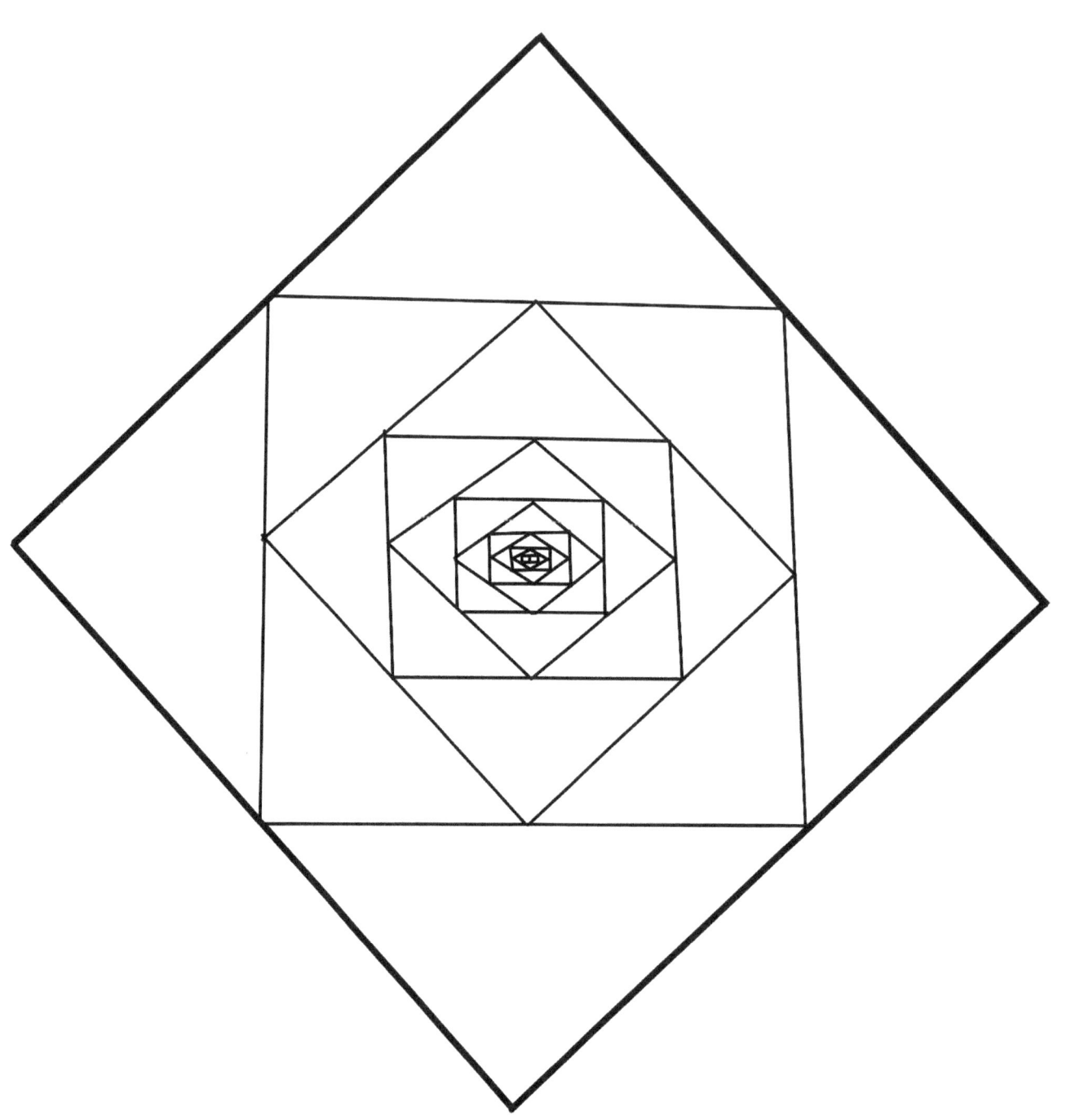

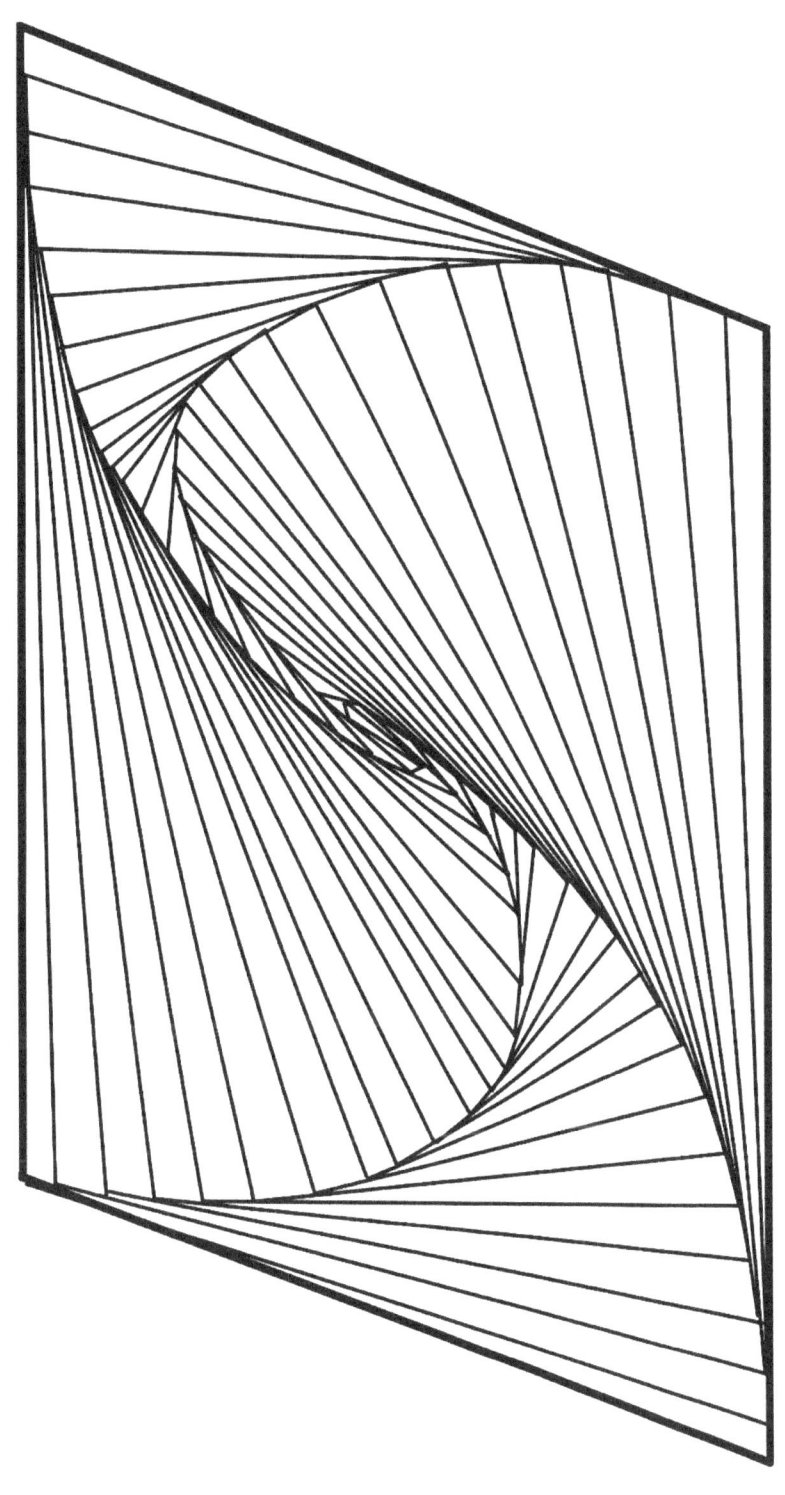

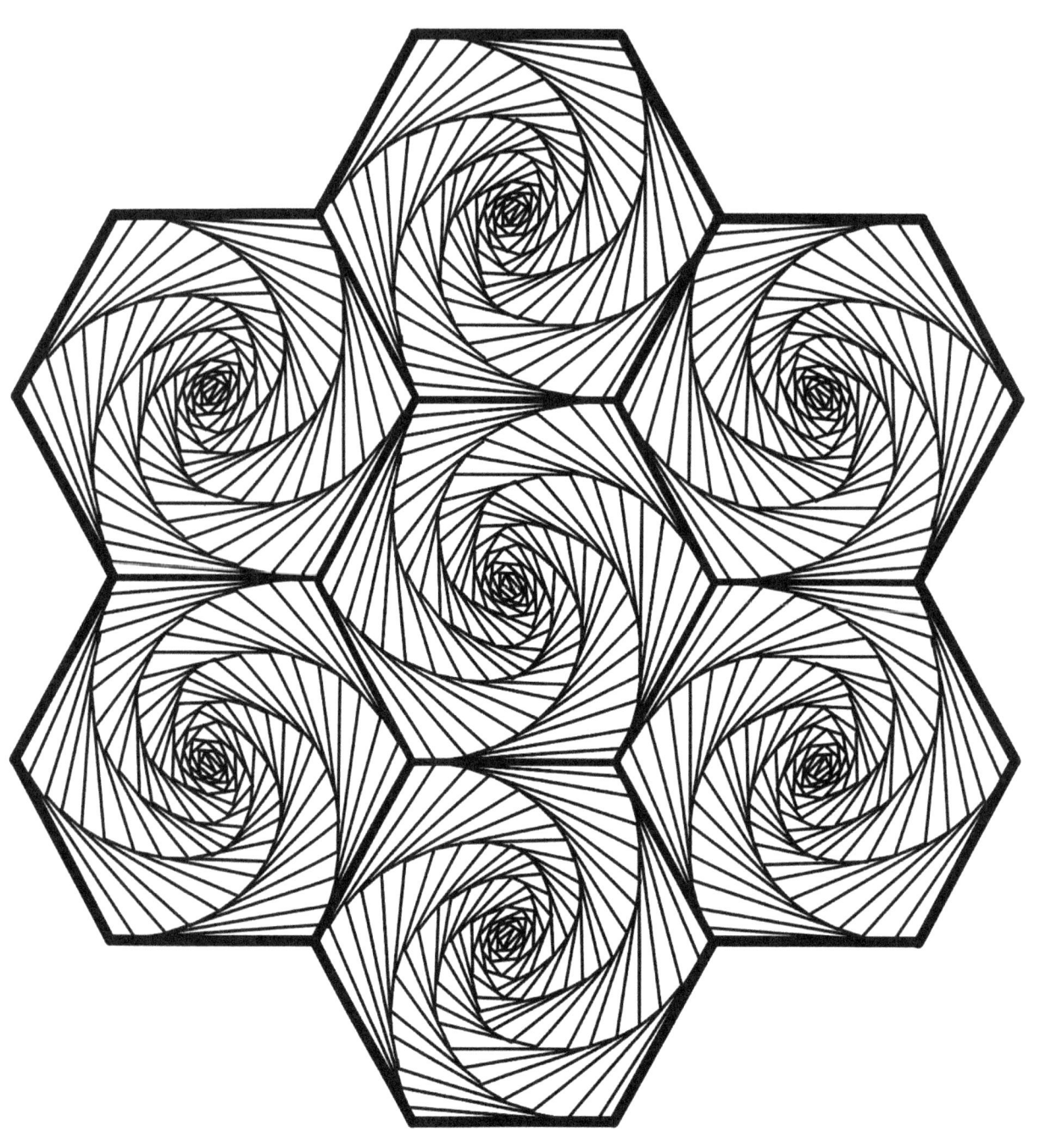

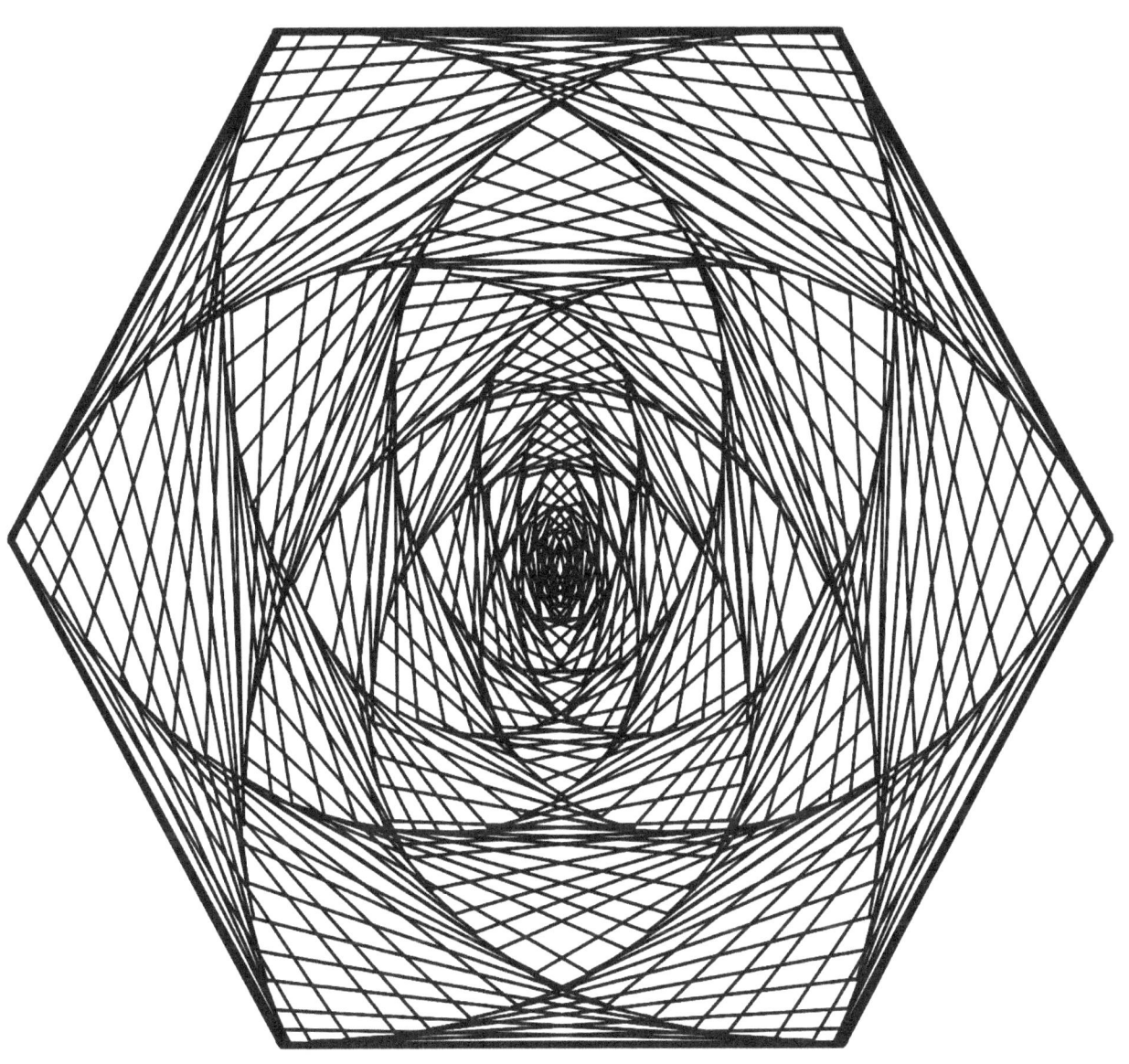

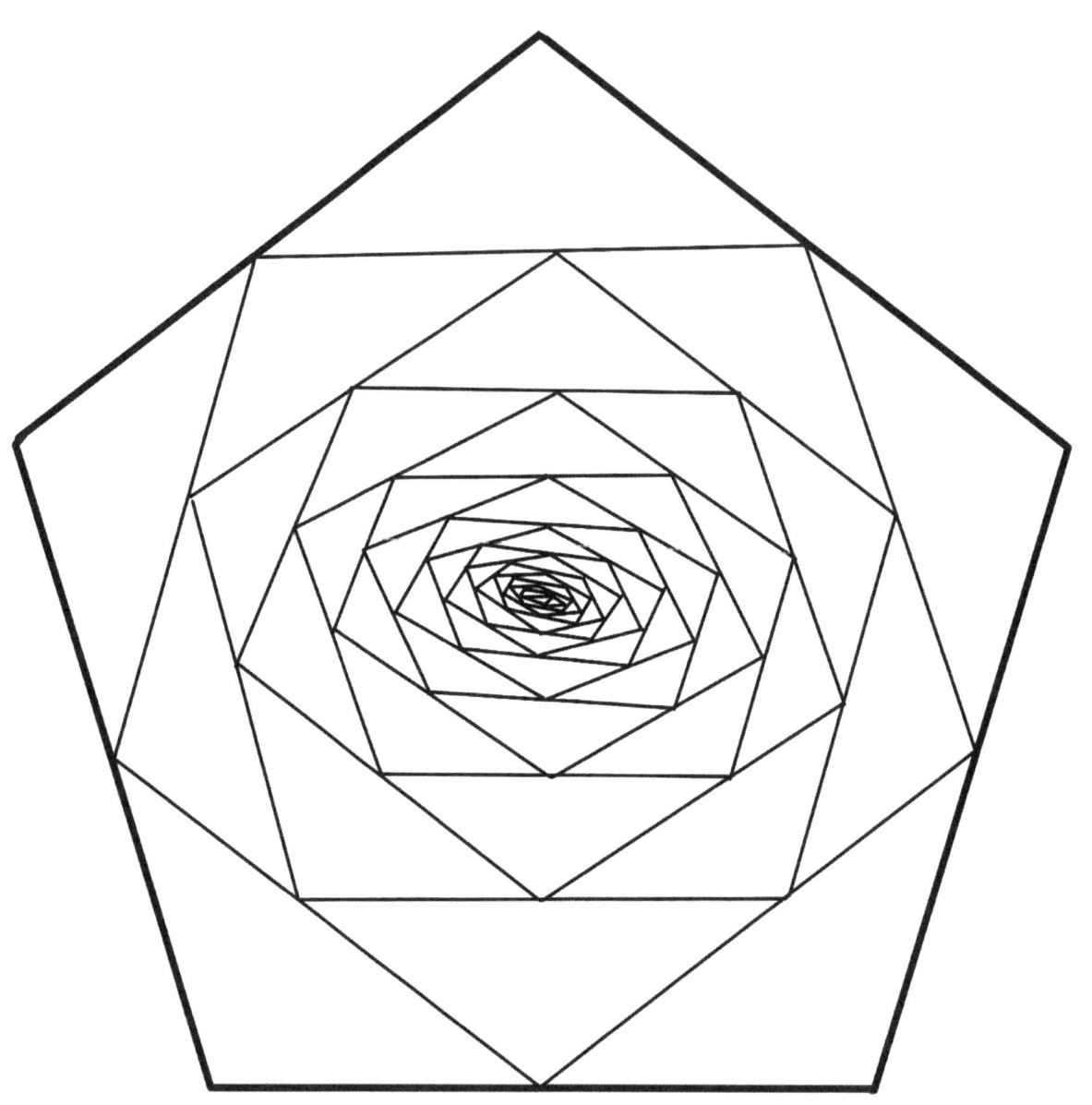

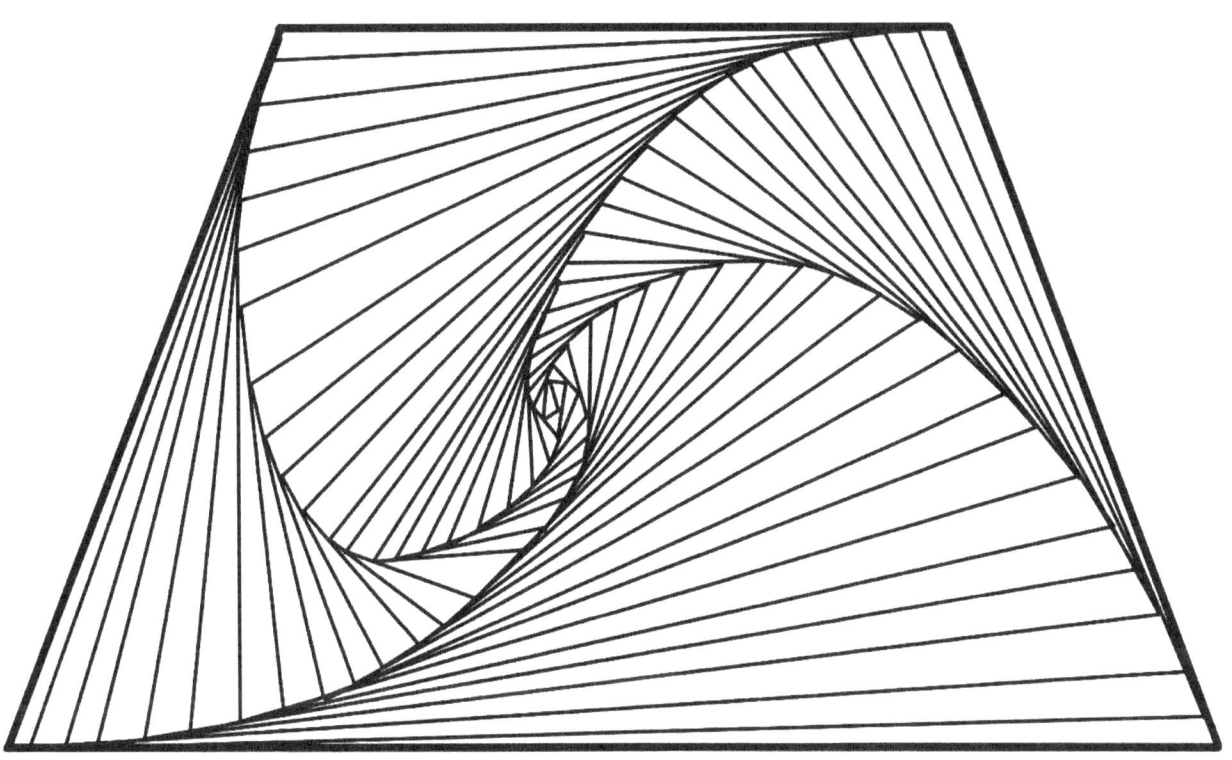

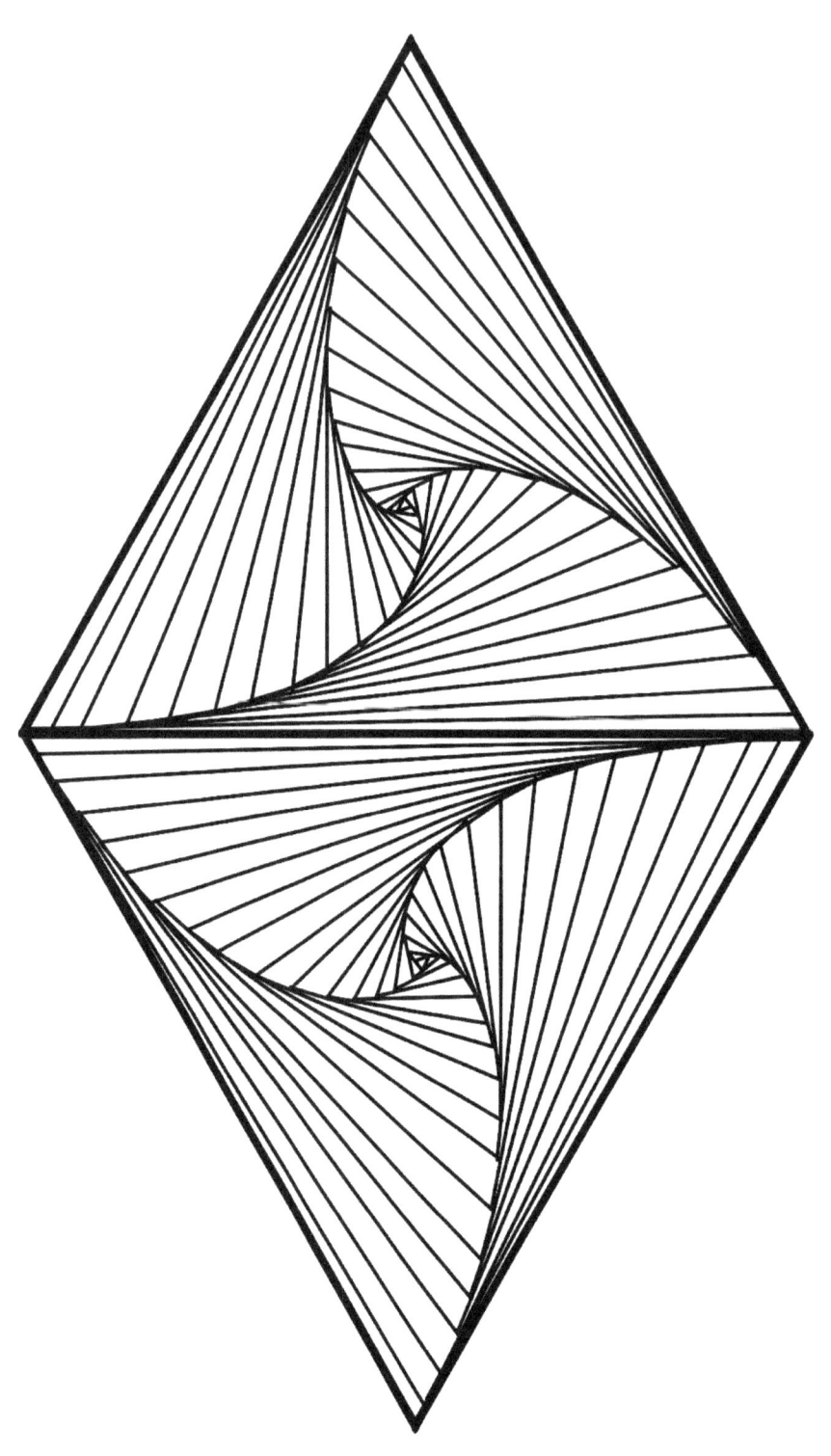

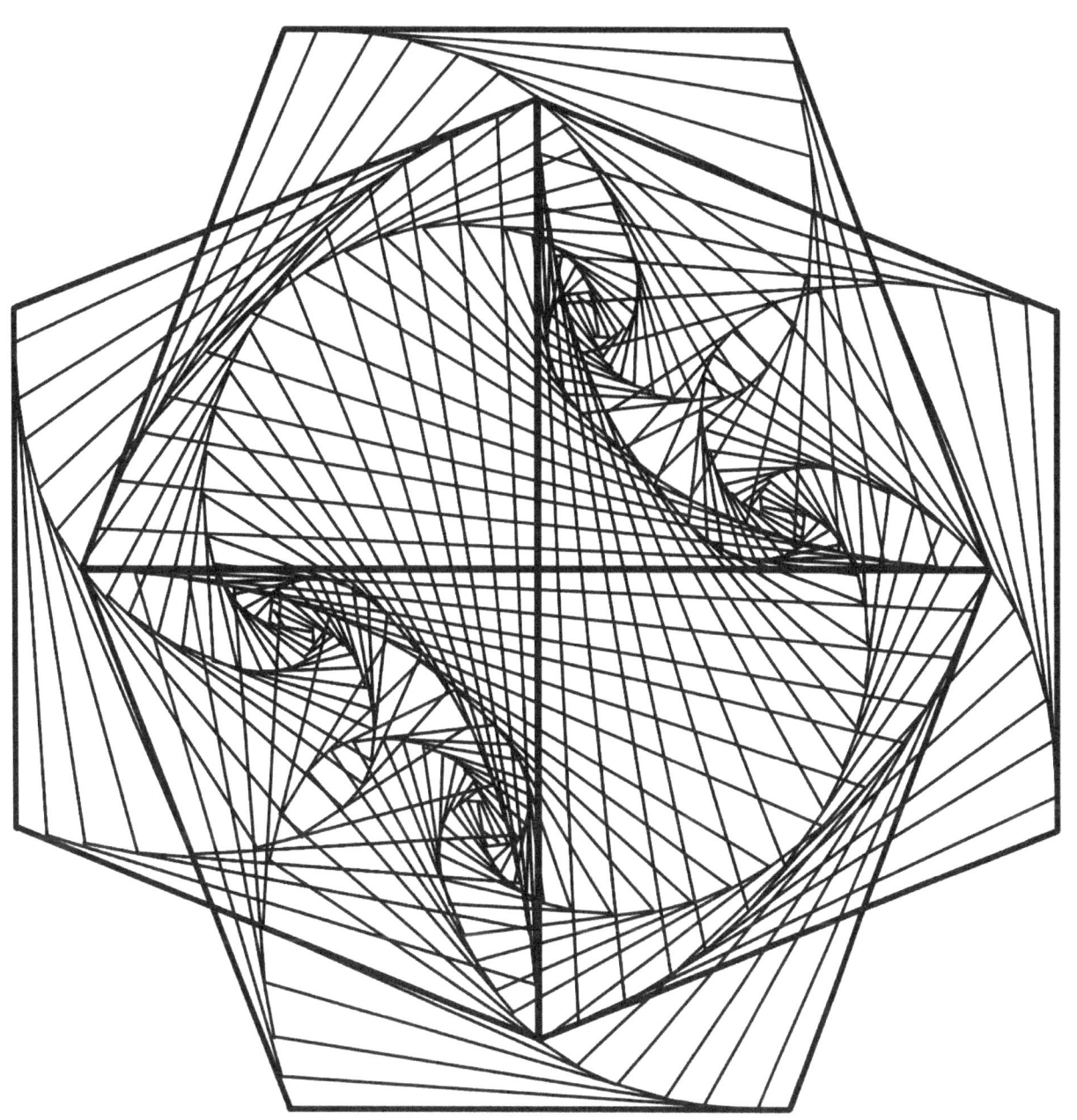

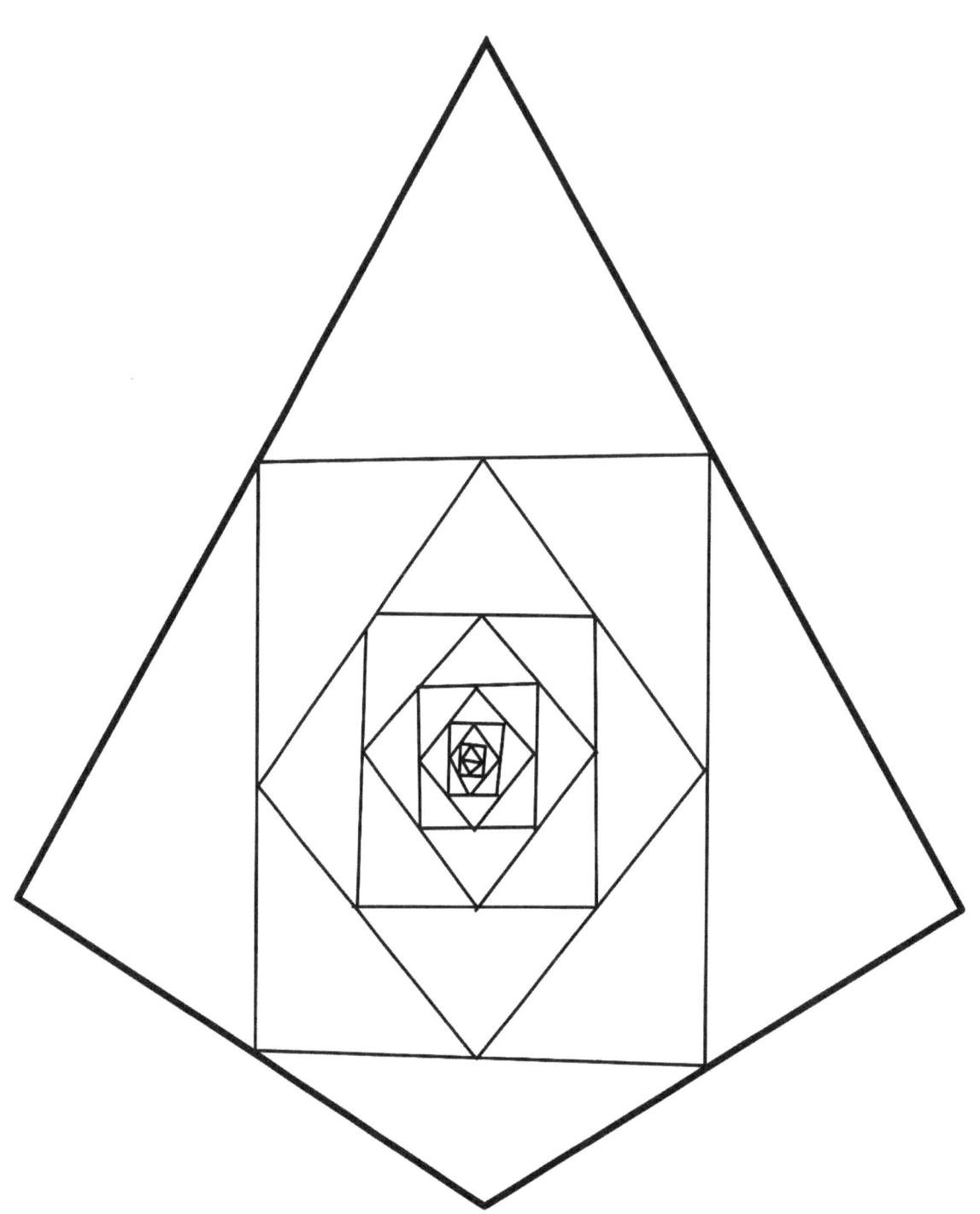

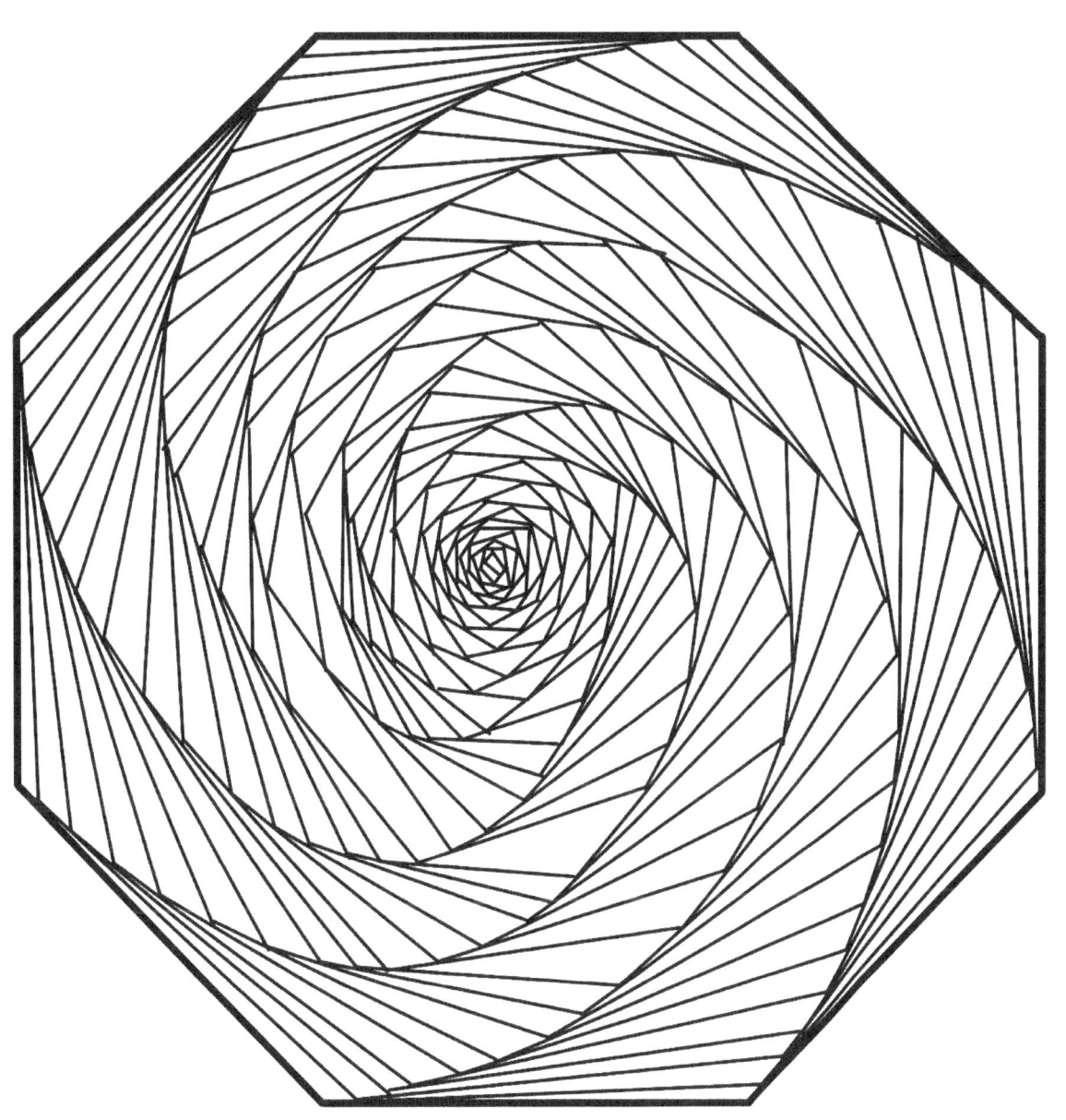

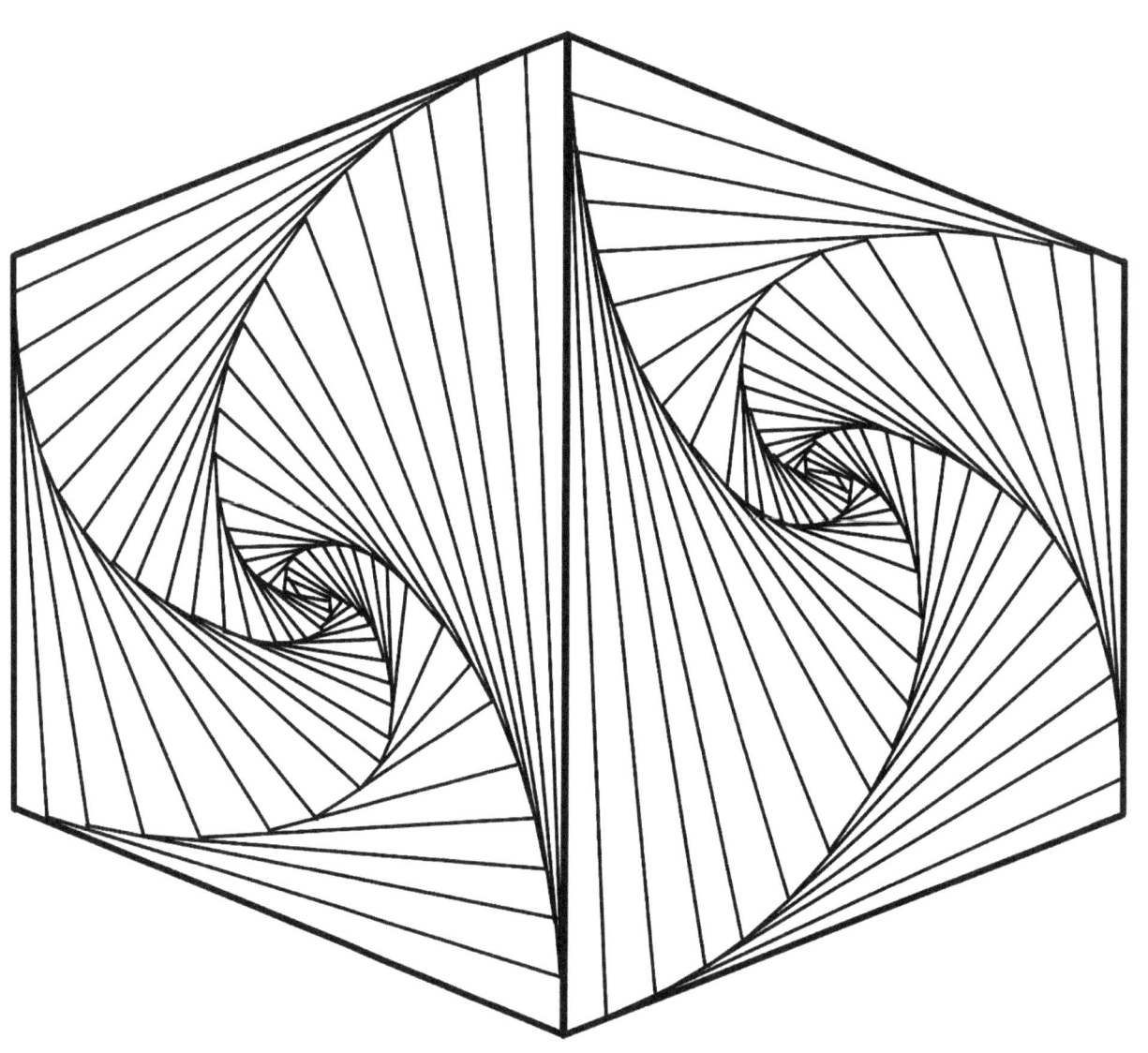

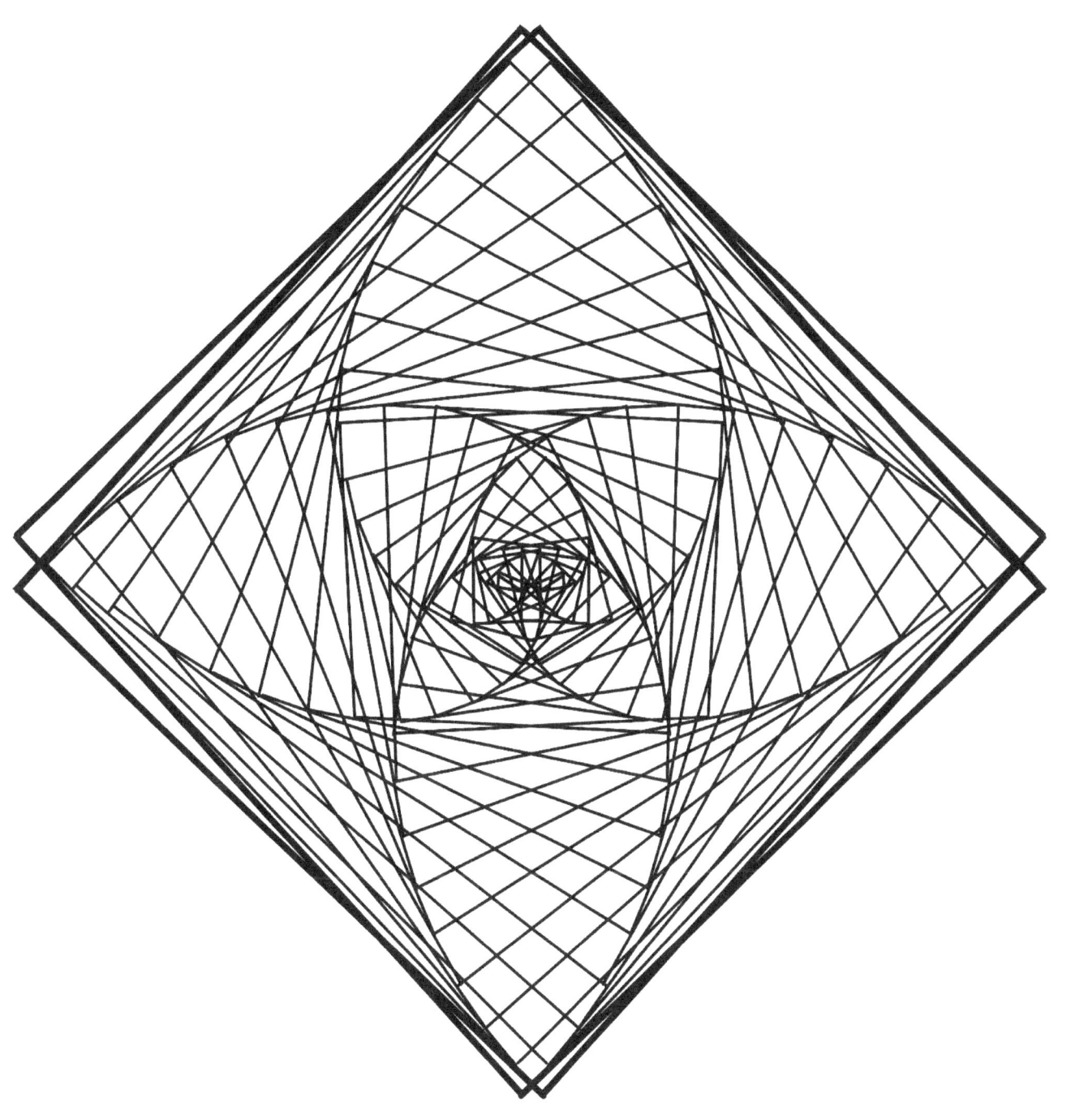

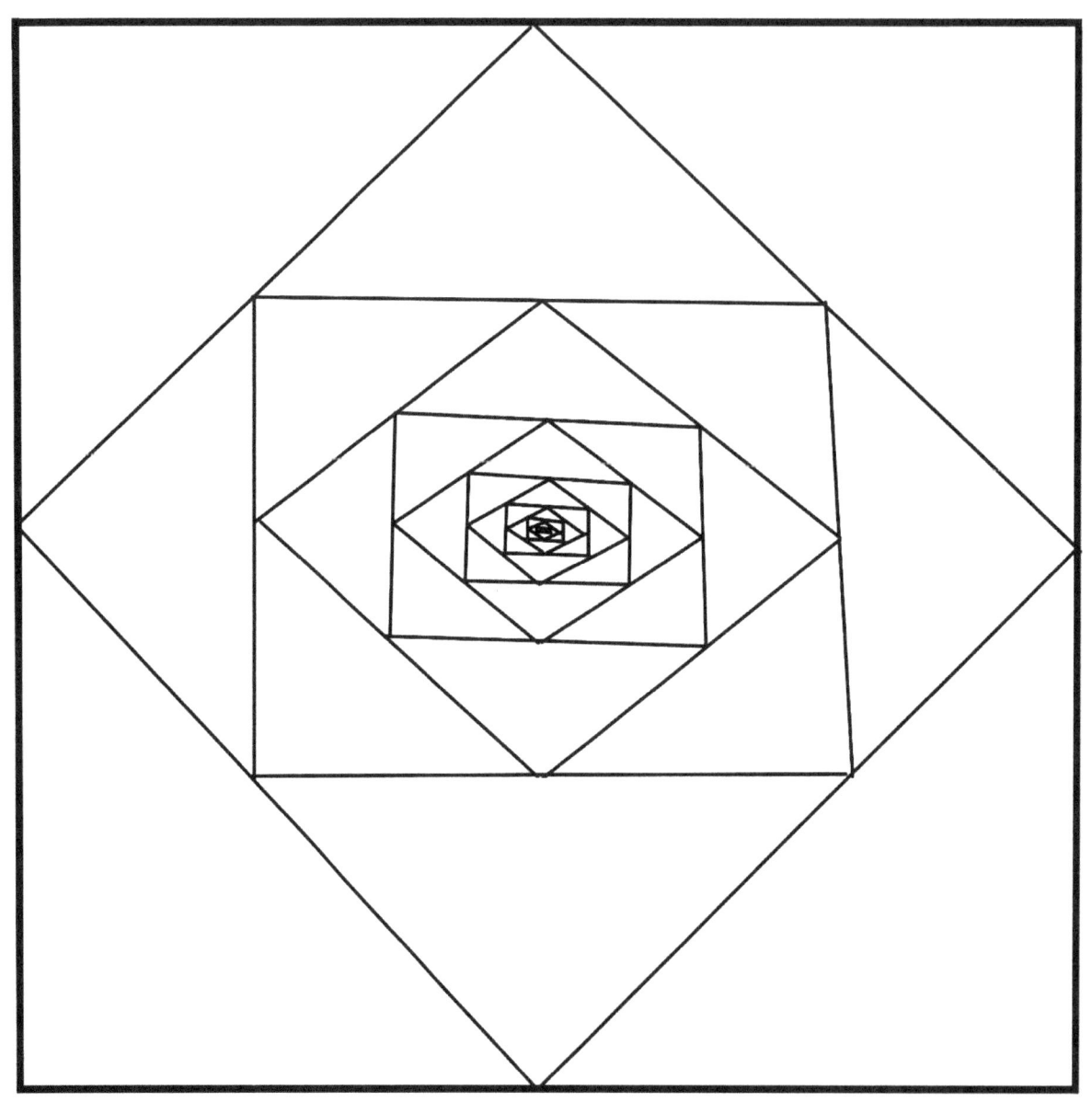

Your Turn!

Now it's your turn to make your own abyssal shapes!

Abyssal Stairs:

1. Start by drawing a basic shape. Squares and triangles are easiest.

2. Pick a corner to start at and draw a line from that corner to the side of another corner.

3. Repeat the process, working your way closer to the center with each line.

 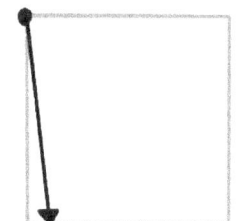 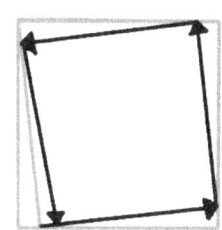

Your lines shouldn't cross over any lines you've drawn previously.

Abyssal Petals:

1. Start by drawing a basic shape. Shapes with 5 or more sides work the best, but squares and triangles are easier.

2. Start at the midpoint of one side and draw a line to the midpoint of an adjacent side. Do this until you are back at your starting point.

3. Once you are back to your starting point, pick a midpoint on the shape you just drew and repteat the process.

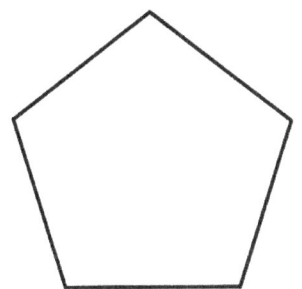 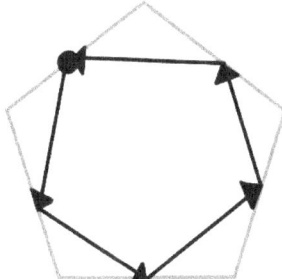 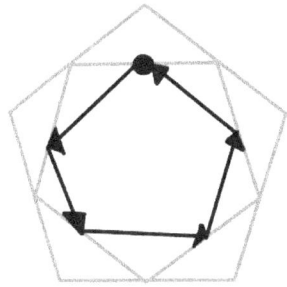

Your shapes will get uneven as you work your way torwards the center, and that's perfectly okay. Now turn the page and practice on the templates!

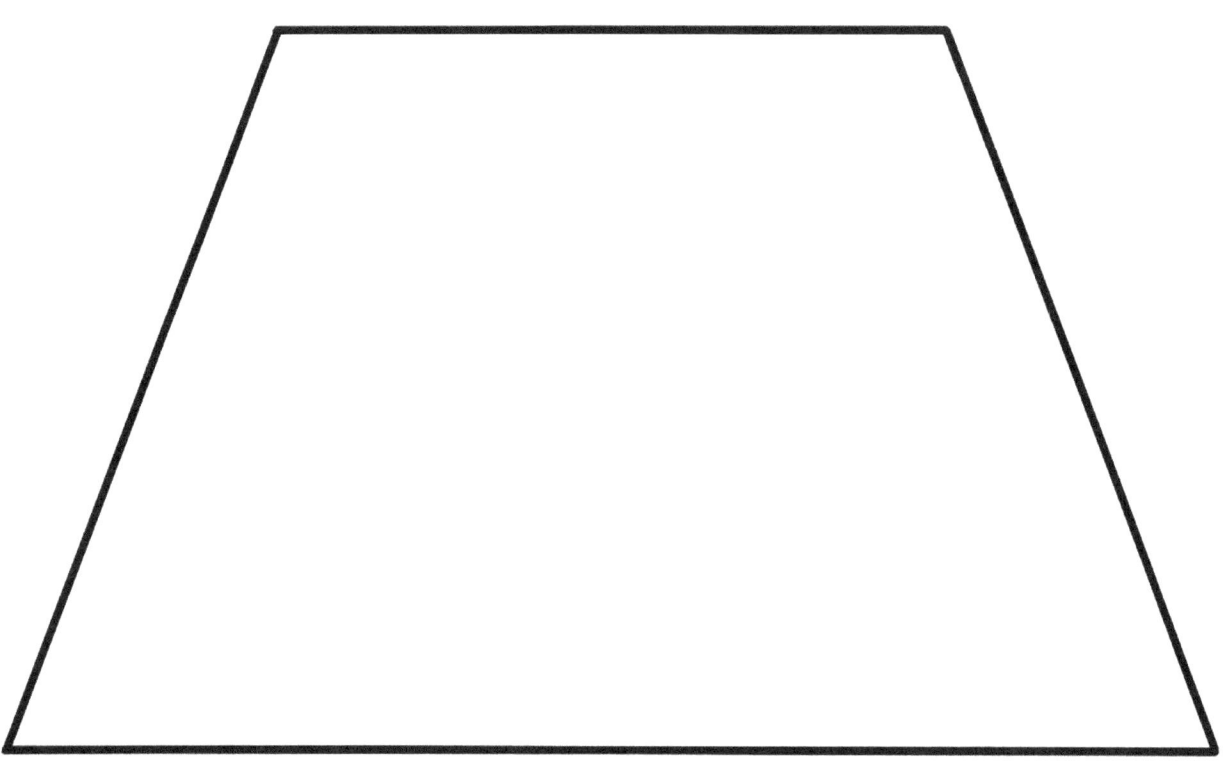

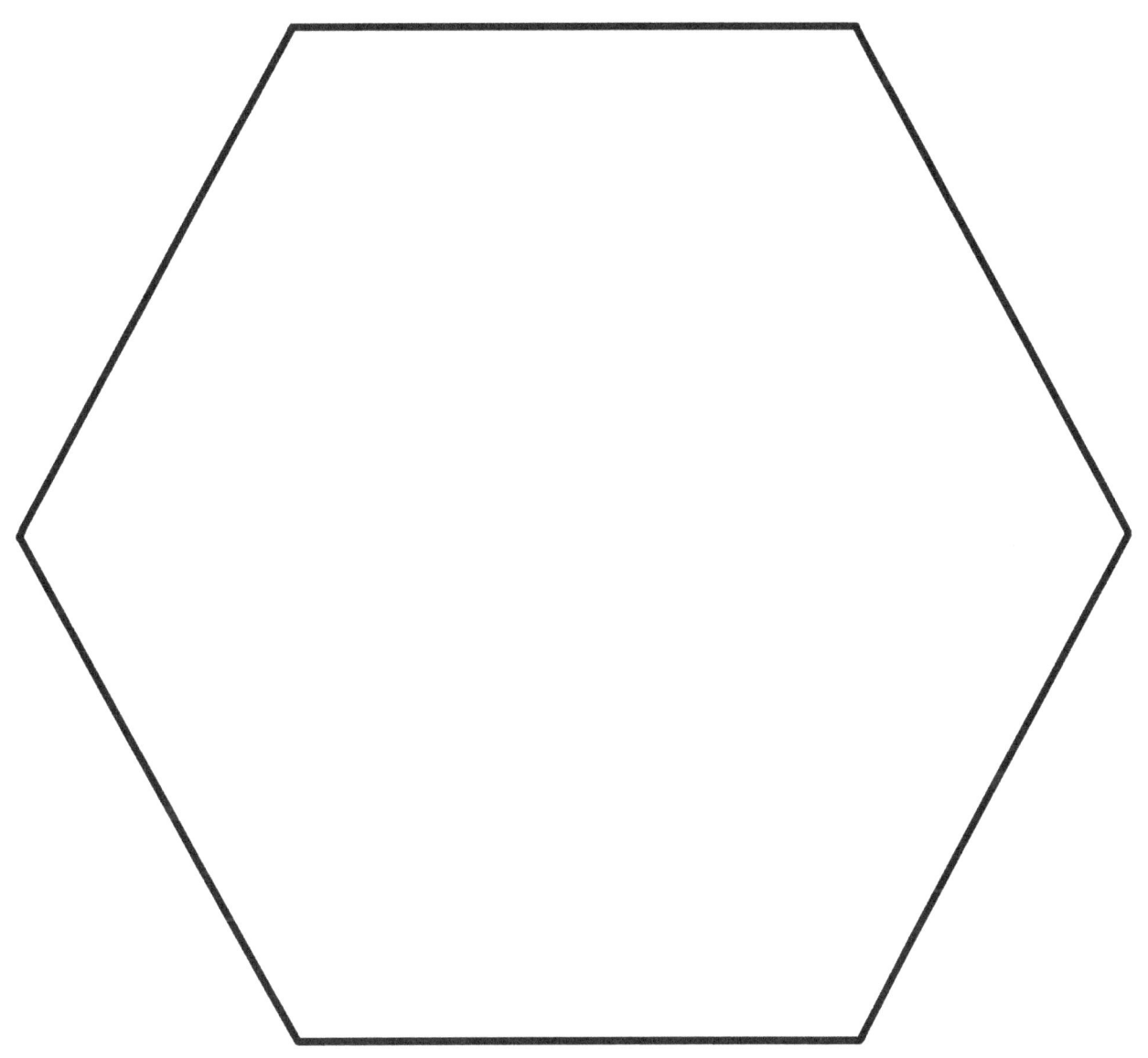

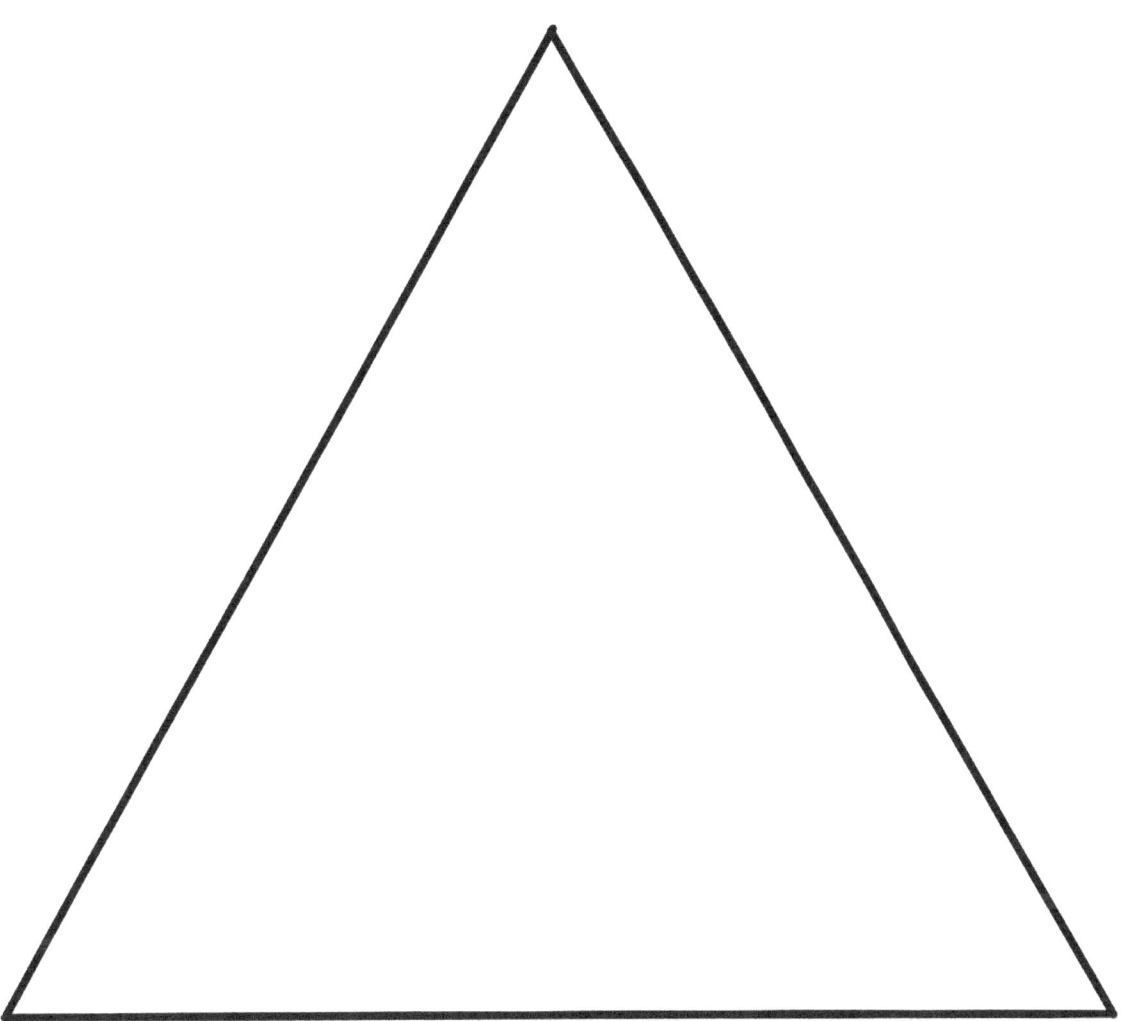

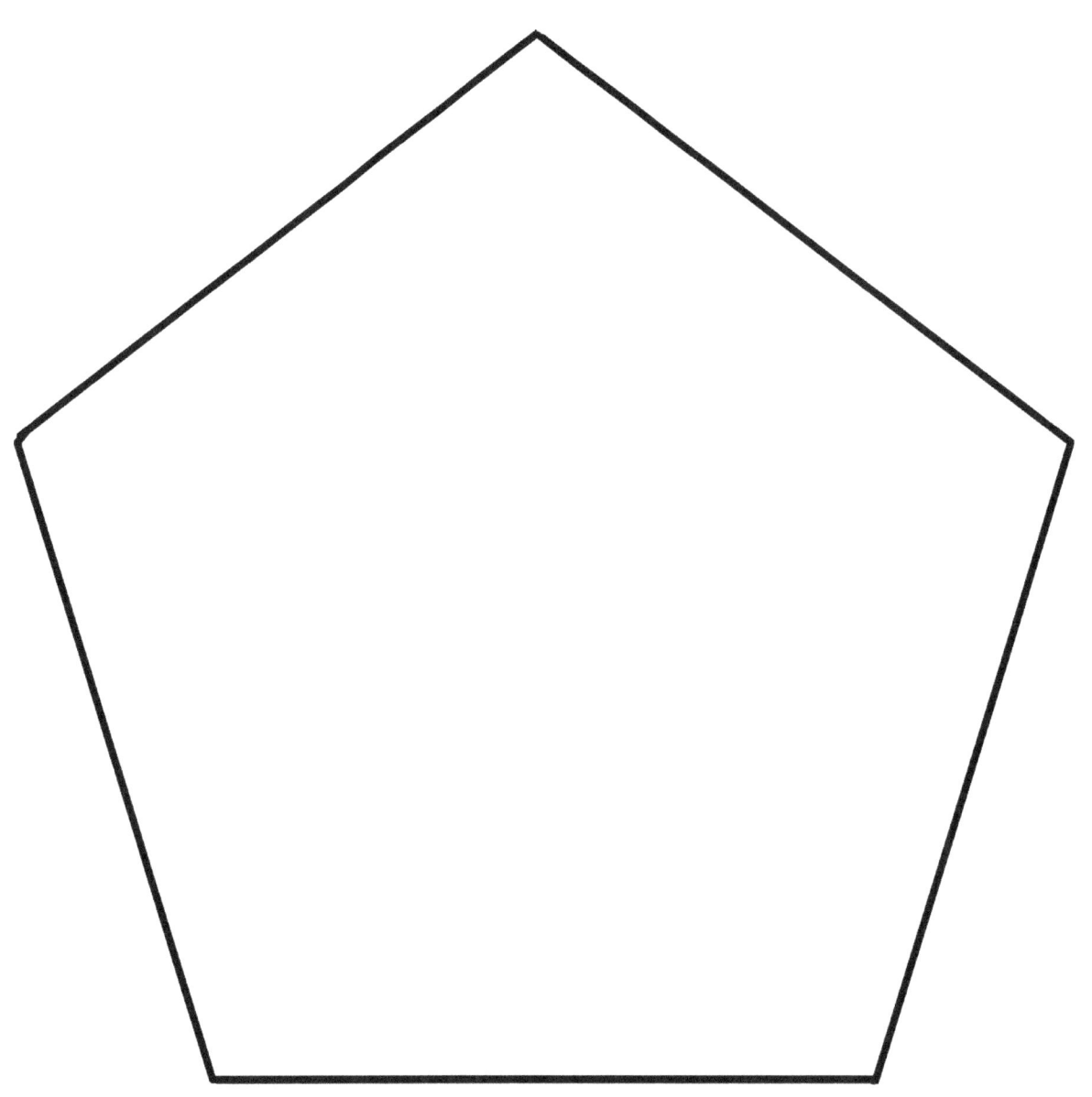

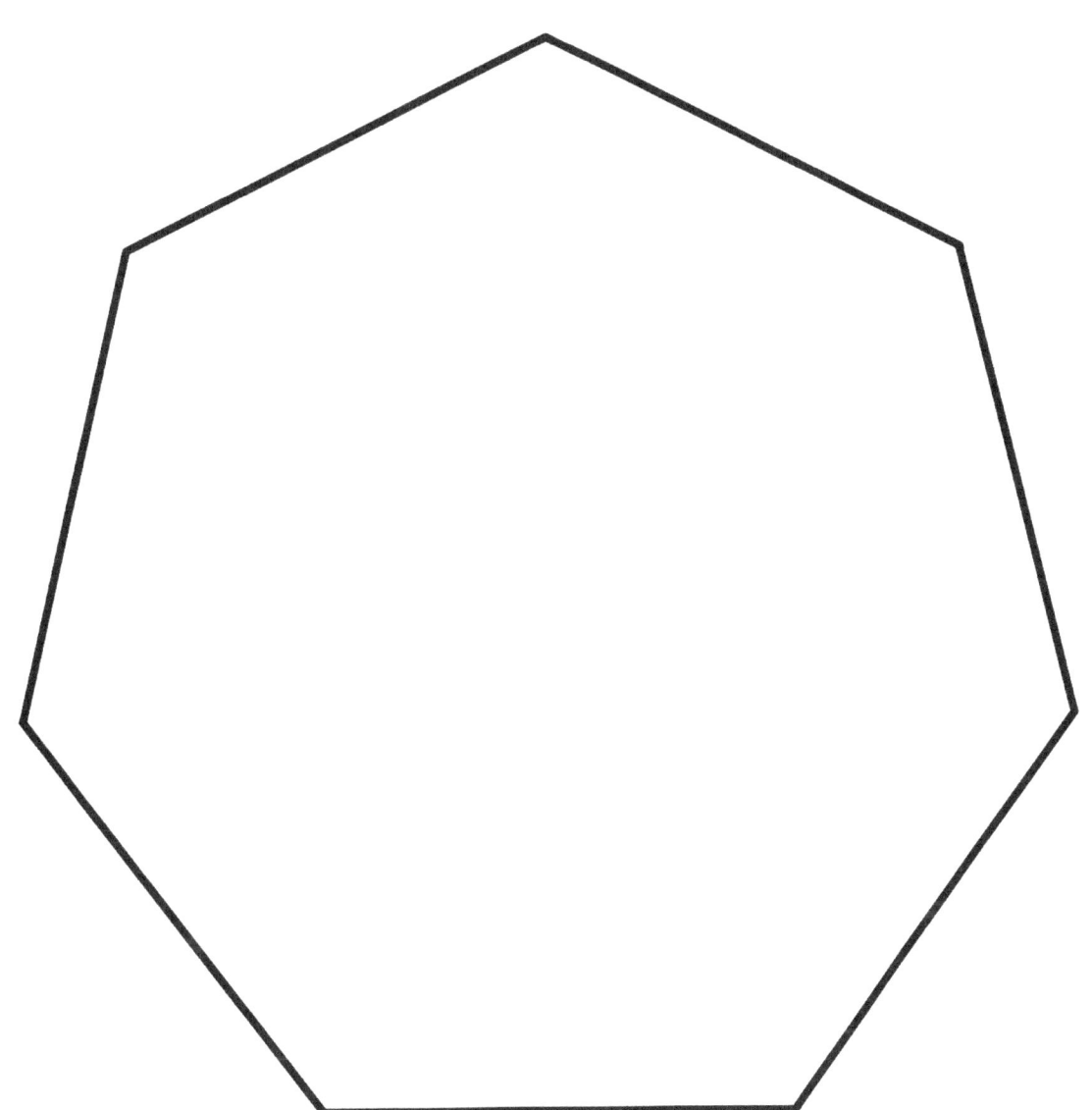

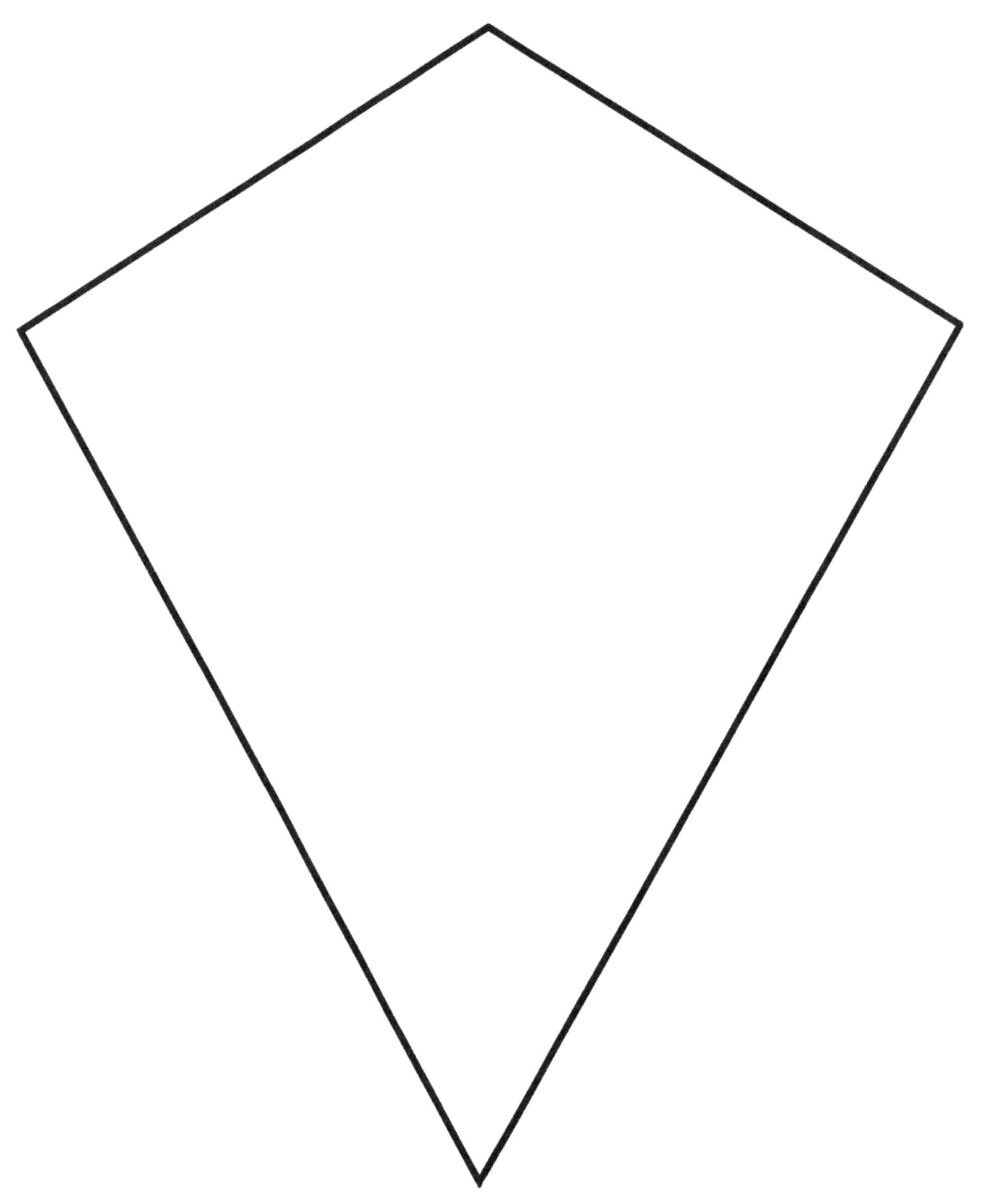

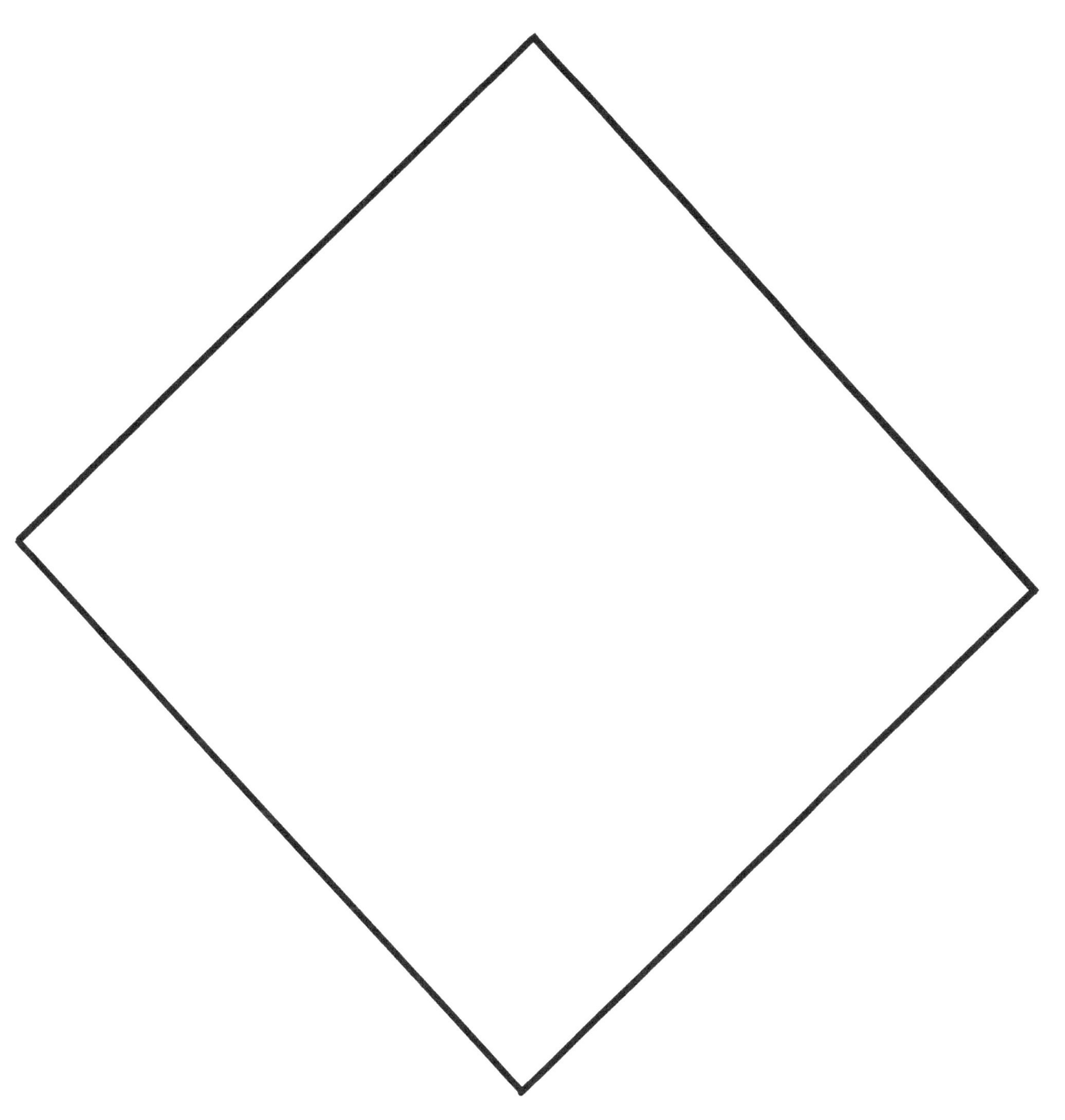

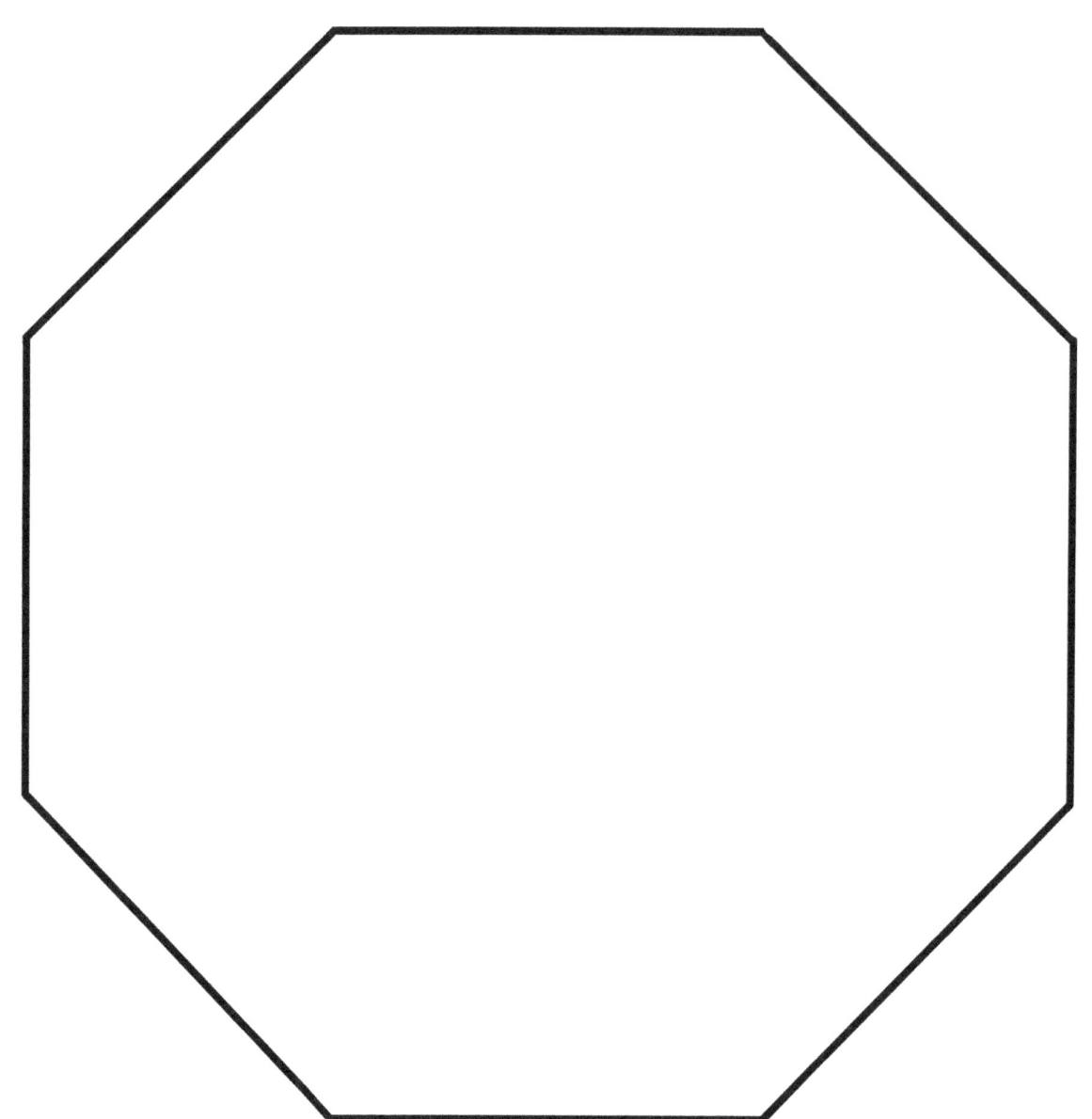

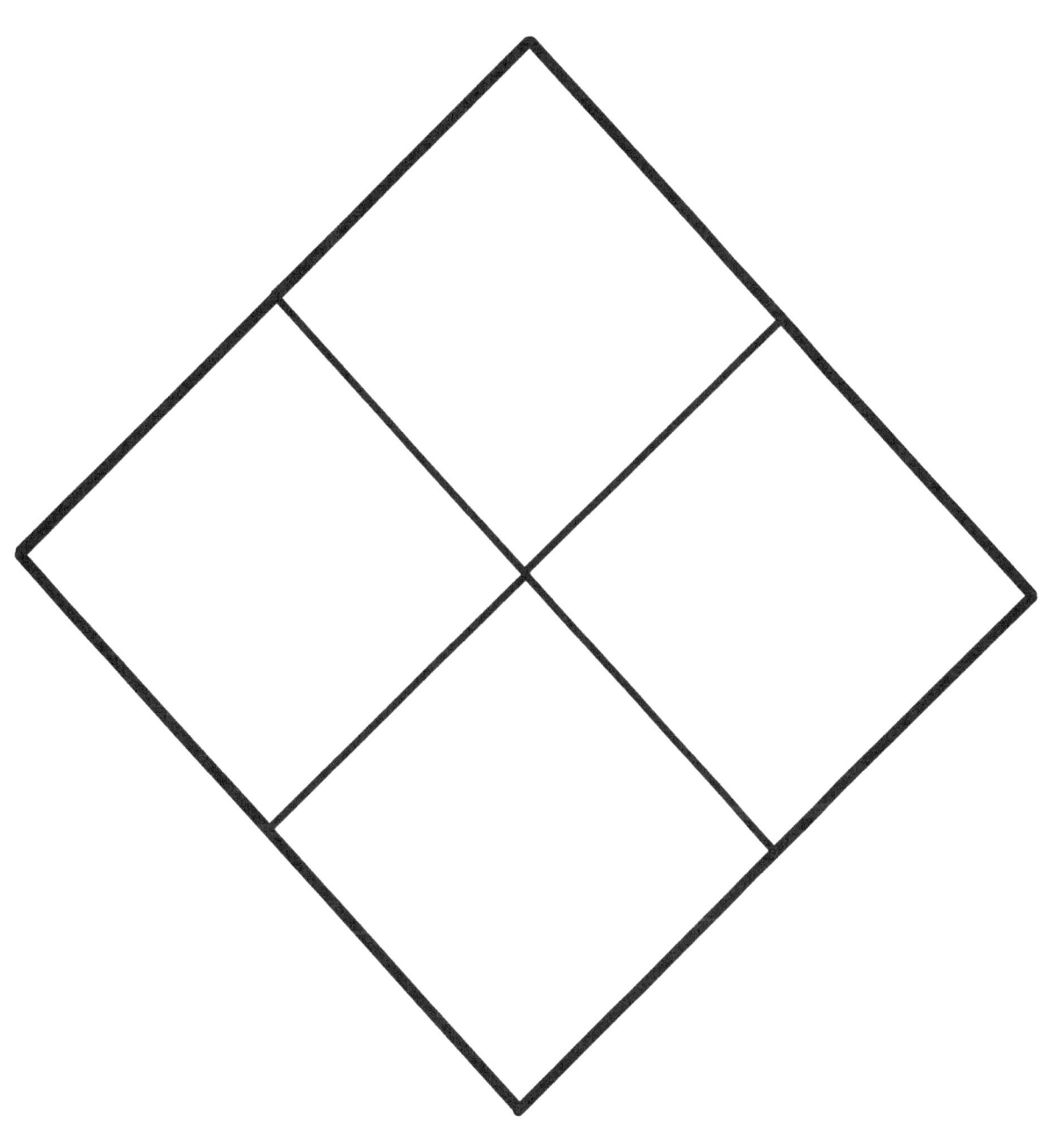

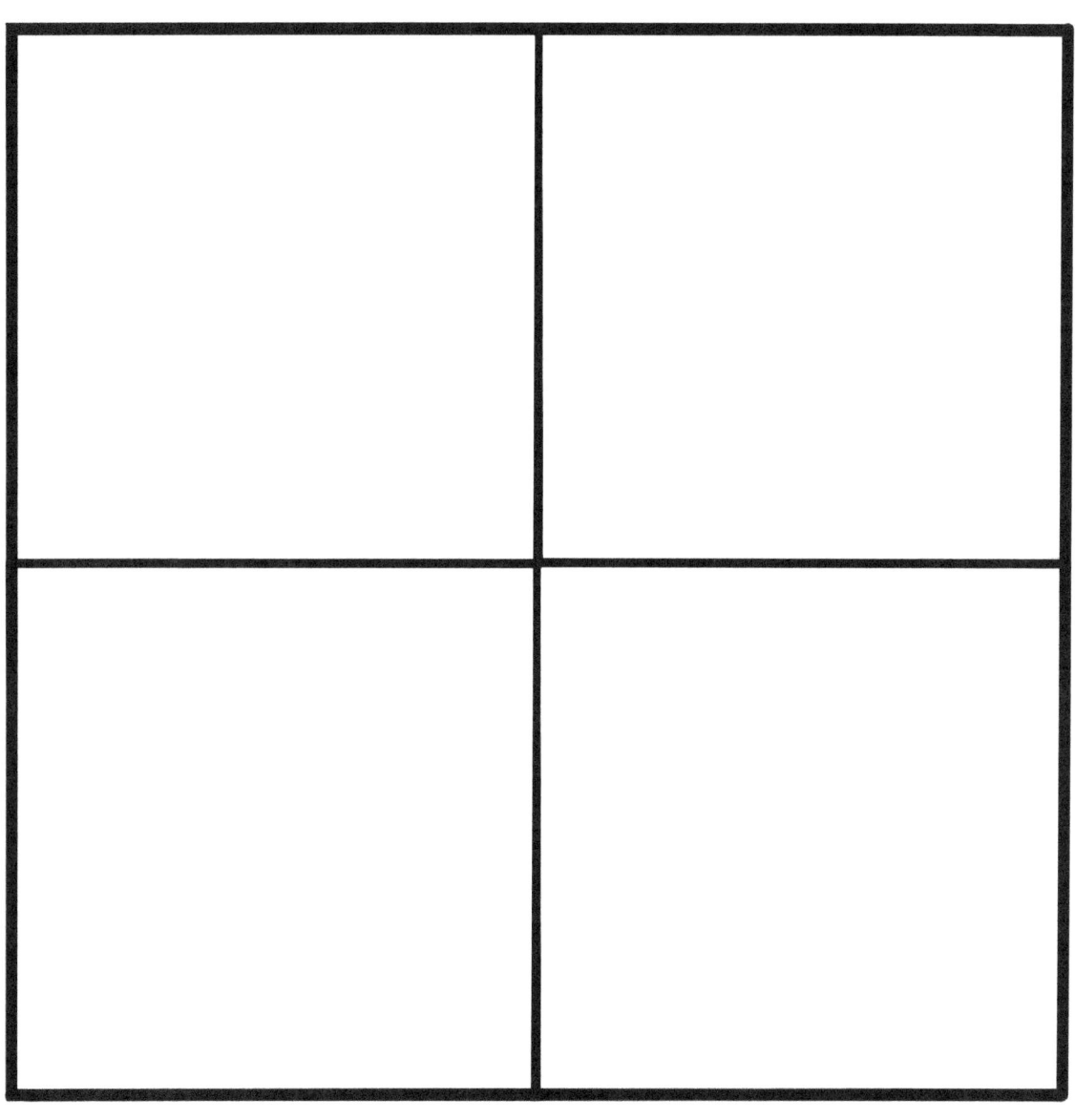

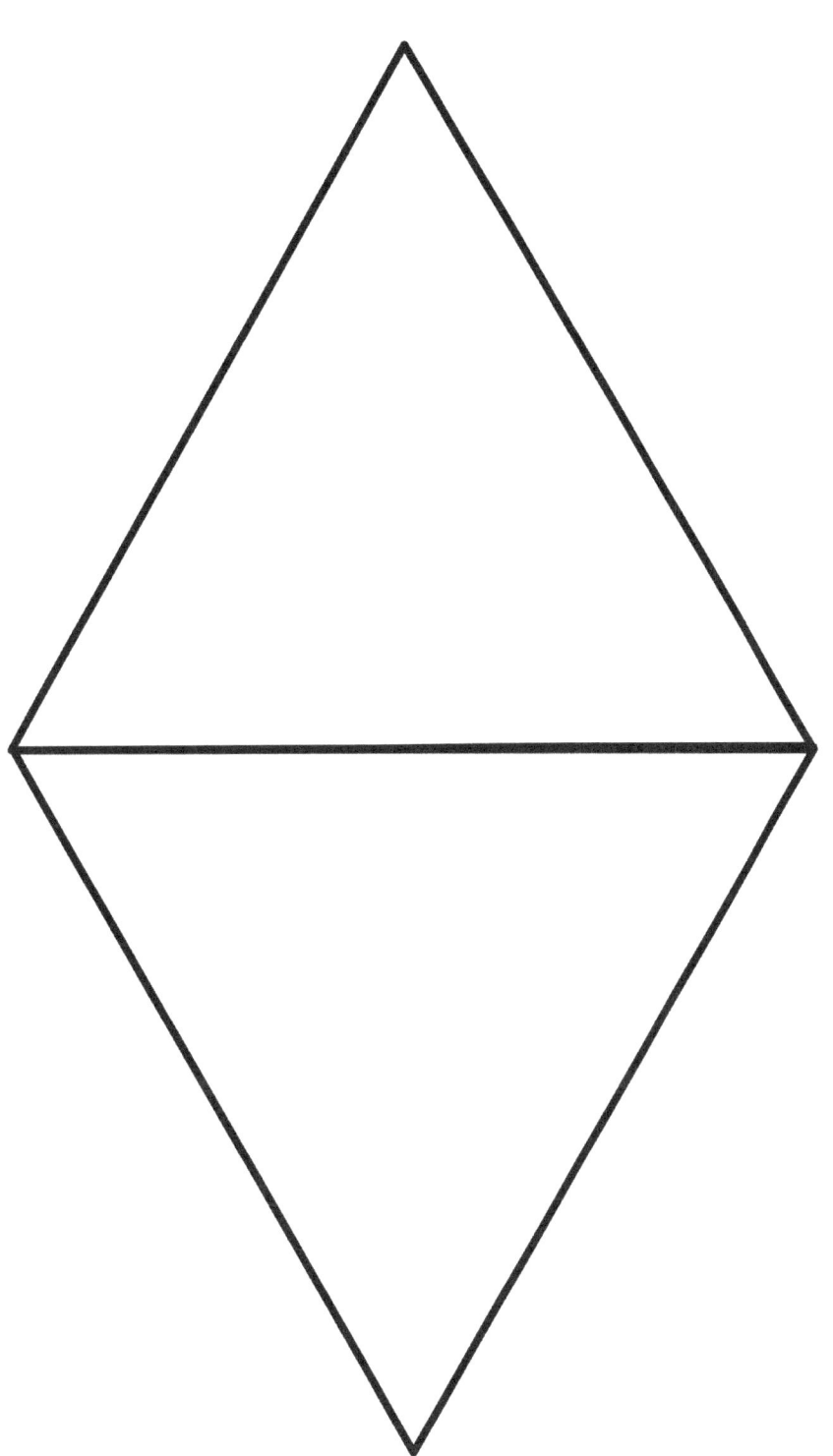